Fashion
in the
Forties
&Fifties

JANE DORNER

LONDON

IAN ALLAN LTD

Contents

Foreword   5

Uniformity and Utility   7

Paris Fashion   27

Britain Can Make It   51

American Casual   79

Teenage Rock   103

Sports Clothes   121

From Top to Toe   143

Acknowledgements   160

Select Bibliography   160

First published 1975

ISBN 0 7110 0584 2   *Casebound edition*
ISBN 0 7110 0585 0   *Paperback edition*

Published by Ian Allan Ltd, Shepperton, Surrey, and printed in the United Kingdom by Ian Allan Printing Ltd

Fashion in the Forties & Fifties

Foreword
by James Laver

What a change has come over histories of costume in the last fifty years! It is true that in the mid 19th century a number of books on the subject were published and some were conscientious and scholarly enough. It was all part of the Romantic Movement, the historicism of an age which applauded the development of neo-Gothic. But the backward look was not always one of admiration, especially in the field of costume. Books were written with such titles as "The Follies of Fashion". Look, they said, at the absurd clothes our ancestors wore – as if the crinolines of 1860 were any less ridiculous than the farthingales of 1600.

Even the scholarly works suffered from certain limitations. The main problem was illustration. No monochrome wood engraving could adequately reproduce the documents of the past, and even chromolithography was not much better. Both processes suffered from the fact that the illustrations had to be redrawn by some contemporary artist. This is never satisfactory, for something of the artist's own period distorts the image. I have myself been surprised by the ease with which I could date, not the original document but the *redrawing*. Photography had not yet come in to help, and of course adequate colour reproduction was quite out of the question. Now all this is changed. In histories of costume photography is extensively used, and colour reproduction has taken an enormous stride forward in the last half century. It is now possible to reproduce, say, a Holbein miniature of Anne of Cleves in all the glory of its original colour.

Then again there has emerged a much more scientific attitude to costume history and there has been a plethora of excellent books on every aspect of the subject. Among these the present work by Jane Dorner must take a distinguished place.

She has limited herself to a couple of recent decades and has thus been able to bring her subject matter nearly up to the present day. In view of the inevitable gap between writing a book and seeing it in print, it is impossible to be *absolutely* up to date. But Jane Dorner has filled a yawning gap in our knowledge by dealing in a masterly way with what happened to clothes during and after World War II.

She tells us of the effects of wartime restrictions and of their gradual relaxation, until Dior's New Look for a time revolutionised female costume. At the height of the new craze I ventured to prophesy that it would not last and that by the mid-fifties women would be back in the post-crisis clothes of the twenties . . .

Miss Dorner deals very informatively with all the influences which flowed in from France, America and Italy, the decline of Haute Couture, the teenage revolution in the United States, the coming of the mini skirt, and the desperate and largely unsuccessful efforts of the dress designers to bring in the 'midi' and the 'maxi'; with the strange aberration of stiletto heels (which are now, I understand, about to return!), with the popularity of the bust-hugging sweater, with the influence of Hollywood, and many other important matters.

But perhaps the most interesting part of the book is its treatment of male costume – a subject largely neglected by historians of fashion. On this subject Miss Dorner has many valuable insights. She distinguishes clearly between neo-Edwardians and the Teddy Boys. The first were concerned to go straight back to the Edwardian period, and the latter to use the new styles for purposes of sexual display – something which no male had thought of since the "great renunciation" of Beau Brummell. She sees that the erotic principle has, for most young men at least, transferred itself back to masculine costume, a revolution of which we are just seeing the beginning. For if women express in their clothes their repudiation of the Patriarchal system, so men's clothes represent a revolt against the 'gentility' which ruled throughout the 19th century and until quite recent years.

Not only specialists but the general public will find in Jane Dorner's book a wealth of information and penetrating ideas. I have certainly learned a lot from it myself.

5

HELP THE R.A.F
JOIN THE WAAF

The WAAF recruiting poster (1940). This poster was withdrawn because the authorities considered that it gave too glamorous an impression of the work involved./*Imperial War Museum*

Uniformity & Utility

In 1940 the New Year edition of *Vogue* declared with the heroic optimism characteristic of wartime journalism: "We put our faith in fashion. In this New Year of war we take this stand and will maintain it against all comers; that fashion is no surface frivolity but a profound instinct; that its pulse beats fast or slow, in time with the march of events but beats with imperishable vitality; that as long as there is taste and coquetry, desire for change and love of self-expression, a sense of fitness and a sense of fantasy – there will be fashion ..." It was a brave assertion, but one not borne out by events, for fashion was halted in its career and stood on the sidelines marking time until the war was well and truly over. Instead of the romantic waspish lines, the sequined furs, the décolletages and the billowing skirts that Paris had promised women only one month before the outbreak of war, came restrained clothing fitting the atmosphere of economy. The wartime picture is one of uniformity and drabness, the atmosphere is austerity and the prevailing attitude is "Make Do and Mend".

To begin with, uniforms were everywhere – in restaurants, at weddings, theatres and gala occasions of all kinds. Never before had the civilian been so keenly aware that there was a war in progress. Men in battledress and women backing their menfolk in the blue, green and khaki uniforms of the auxiliary forces were to be seen everywhere. Women who did not wear uniform hardly dared to flaunt themselves in frivolous costumes: the fox furs, veils, lace and inconsequential posies they had donned before the outbreak of war now seemed in bad taste. The silhouette was unadorned, a plain rectangle of clothing consisting of a box-shaped jacket with padded shoulders and a narrow skirt. Even summer dresses and blouses had shoulder pads and conformed to the severity of outline demanded by wartime deprivation. Cecil Beaton said at the time that women's fashions were going through the Beau Brummell stage and were learning the restraint of men's taste.

Restraint and practicability were the yardsticks against which fashion was measured. Women wanted clothing that would allow them freedom of movement and fortify them against unpredictable occurrences. This accounts for the popularity of ample hooded cloaks in which they could sleep out if necessary, kangaroo pockets they could hurriedly fill with treasured possessions, and clumpy wedge-soled shoes that imparted a feeling of confidence that they could walk for miles. Above all, the siren suit responded to a profound need for body and mind to be warmly, safely protected from fear and danger. This enveloping garment, which could be zipped on as its wearer dashed to the air-raid shelter, was worn by all from Winston Churchill to the kitchen-maid, and expressed the social equalization occurring at a time when common experiences neutralized class barriers. It was one of the few fashions born out of a need for practicality to remain in the fashion designers' repertoire, for it graduated to become slinky hostess wear in later years.

Another popular style that reduced all wearers to a common denominator of simplicity was the turban, which had begun as a safety device to keep hair out of factory machines but was rapidly adopted by the working woman seeking a quick disguise but with no time for a lengthy hairdo. In Paris, where the fashion collections still showed the fanciful, the designer Agnès came out with a curious red and blue turban that bandaged the jaw but left the head bare. This uncomfortable piece of headgear boldly flaunted its patriotism – but its inspiration came from first aid.

Britain, France, and even the United States each coped differently with wartime restrictions. United States designers tried to launch a return to the twenties fashions that had fitted the mood after the First World War, with tubular skirts in neutral shades, cloche hats and a feeling of unadorned simplicity; Paris was on the track of something more feminine – small waists, full skirts, sloping shoulders; England opted for square uniformity. But all agreed with the Paris dictum "*Il faut* skimp *pour être chic*". This was of course making a virtue out of necessity, the shortage of cloth was world wide and rationing allowed for little versatility.

7

Rationing in Britain operated on a strict coupon system that was announced in the pages of women's magazines in 1941. At first sixty-six coupons per year were allocated, but the number dropped to forty-eight and finally to thirty-six in the last year of the war. Designers concentrated on a bias cut, which lent restrained fullness to the silhouette and hinted at more than was really there. There was no cloth to spare for pockets and pleats and no time to waste on fancy stitching, buttons and trimmings. Government restrictions in Britain made it illegal to squander labour on decoration in regulations that harked back to the sumptuary laws of the Middle Ages which were enforced with some severity. One West End dressmaker even found herself in court for no greater crime than embroidering butterflies on to a pair of cami-knickers.

Such exceptions were uncommon, as most members of the fashion trade were eager to co-operate on government clothing policy and leading designers such as Norman Hartnell, Captain Molyneux, Charles Creed and Hardy Amies did their bit for the war effort by creating utility clothing (stamped with the official approval sign CC41) for the Board of Trade. In the United States, too, the top couturier, Main-bocher, gave advice on cutting to save cloth and designed uniforms for service women, who were soon being envied by European sisters for their elegance. Manufacturers in the States laboured under the Limitation Order L-85, which was enforced by the War Production Board. In France the situation was slightly different, since after the fall of Paris in 1940 the couture industry was technically in the hands of the Germans. Lucien Lelong, President of the Chambre Syndicale de la Couture Parisienne, did manage to obtain exemption from textile rationing for the top twelve couture houses (see Chapter 2), but their aim was in fact to waste the precious cloth, not to save it, since profits only went to swell the pockets of the enemy. The resulting designs, with voluminous skirts and sleeves, naturally ran counter to the interests of countries who were trying to save cloth, so when pictures of the Paris fashions appeared in *Vogue* immediately after the war, the War Production Board of America tried to encourage press censorship. They saw the new styles as an "unhealthy condition in the women's apparel field . . . The constant flow of pictures showing clothes so diametrically the opposite of ours cannot help but stir interest in the new and entirely different looking silhouette." American resentment was particularly acute, for while the smartest Parisiennes were flaunting extravagantly wasteful dresses, the French government was simultaneously trying to import American manufactured clothes as there was a shortage of garments for ordinary people. Clearly the American authorities were anxious that the Parisian silhouette should be kept to a minimum.

Clothes rationing lasted until 1949. Making the coupons stretch represented a jigsaw puzzle that required all a woman's ingenuity, especially when she had to break into her personal allowance to clothe her growing youngsters. For adult women the following number of coupons applied:

Utility tweed suits	18
Coats	14
Jackets	11
Woollen dresses	11
Dresses in other fabrics	7
Blouses, cardigans, jumpers	5
Skirts	7
Overalls, jumpsuits	6
Pyjamas	8
Stockings	2
2 Handkerchiefs	1
2 oz, knitting wool	1

Stockings were so expensive on coupons and so scarce that regulations specified the wearing of socks in summer. Necessity, the mother of invention, produced an attempt by some women to paint their legs tan to look as if they were wearing stockings.

In the middle years of the war, when the rate was fixed at forty-eight clothing coupons, a man could buy a pair of socks every four months, a pair of shoes every eight months, a shirt every twenty months, a vest and pair of underpants every two years, a waistcoat every five years, a pullover every five years and an overcoat every seven years. This left three coupons a year for odd items such as handkerchiefs. Clothing was classified according to the amount of cloth or yarn used in its manufacture, with pure wool rated highest, but the restrictions imposed on manufacturers led to such a lowering of standards that the customer was not only forced to buy rarely, but he could not even rely on his garments standing up to the test of time.

There were, of course, ways of stretching one's coupons. Blankets, for example, were not rationed, so they could be dyed and used to make a snug coat. A decorative pillowcase could be combined with lace, which was not rationed, to make a pretty blouse. Women's magazines were full of ideas for refashioning old clothes and the big stores opened departments where they could be mended or made up into new garments. An old swagger coat, for example, could easily be converted into a new suit, while a pair of man's grey flannels would make a tailored skirt. Women's resources of inventiveness were endless and the slogan "Make Do and Mend" (which those who lived through those years probably never want to hear again) neatly summed up a nation's clothing problems.

The mainspring of the young woman's genius for improvisation was her irrepressible desire for simple femininity and the urge to enchant the serviceman on leave. Fabric design boomed, producing a mass of pretty prints, some of them saucily patriotic. Designs embraced jaunty military flags emblazoned with the words "England expects every man to do his duty"; frocks were strewn with the words "Happy landing"; "Free France" and "Dig for Victory". The actress Vivien Leigh boldly wore a 66-coupon blouse with things rare and rationed printed all over it. A note of gaiety could be struck with carefully chosen accessories which were not rationed for most of the war years. But such extras were extremely hard to find and a favourite hat had to last through many a formal occasion.

An additional trial for the fashion-conscious British woman was that she was made tantilizingly aware of what her richer American sisters were wearing. *Vogue* and *Harper's Bazaar* (copies of which were passed from reader to reader) carried seemingly endless series of pictures of the latest styles which appeared in the collections of the newly formed Incorporated Society of London Fashion Designers who had banded together to increase Britain's export trade. An exhibition of dolls wearing the spangled and ruffled gowns that the queen wore in peacetime was sent to the States as a reminder to American buyers that since France had fallen in 1940, Britain was making fashion news. The message went out that Americans could help the war effort by buying from London. The response was immense and "Buy British" shops sprang up in New York. The efforts of the British actress Gertrude Lawrence, who had been living in the States for many years, typified the mood. She undertook to raise $1,000 (£250*) by herself, sewing pyjamas, making gramophone records for the forces, persuading her friends and neighbours to start knitting and selling British emblems.

At the same time American designers began to capitalize on their own resources and looked for inspiration from within the continent. Pretty summer frocks costing about $1 (about 25p), with frills and flounces influenced by neighbouring Mexico, were worn all through the war years. Separates and sports clothes began their fashion career on the beaches of California, where girls wore fresh cotton blouses with miners' levi pants – a fashion that was to have a tremendous influence after the war, when the flow of ideas across the Atlantic became two-way.

After their long period of isolation, Americans in postwar Europe, in official and unofficial guise, had a freshly minted, larger-than-life appearance that contrasted sharply with the battered look Europeans were acquiring. American GIs with gifts of nylon stockings

*Conversion is based on the exchange rate of the time, viz: $4 to the £ up to 1949, $2.8 to the £ thereafter.

ousted home-grown boy-friends in feminine popularity polls, for in spite of the Board of Trade's insistence that they were luxury items, there was a feverish and unremitting pursuit of nylons. A rumour that a store had received a consignment would conjure up queues thousands long for a small stock that would melt away in minutes.

For home-coming servicemen the prospect of finding comfortable clothing seemed equally bleak. They were issued with a "demob suit", a shirt, two collars, two pairs of socks, one pair of shoes and a pair of cufflinks, a tie and a hat, often badly made out of second-rate materials. Replacing a shirt involved a lengthy search for the right size and a five week wait for it to be laundered was by no means unusual. The stark reality was in marked contrast to the expectations expressed in the lines of the soldier song "When I get my civvy clothes on/Oh how happy I shall be!", and many found re-adjustment to civilian life more difficult than they had imagined. By 1946 familiarity with the language of economic beleaguerment – "Austerity Now for Stability Later", "Equality of Sacrifice", "Economic Dunkirk" – was beginning to jar on the nerves of the British public. Prosperity was, however, on the increase and rationing was becoming less severe. Women were eager to express their hopes for a return to normal life in dress that was less austere. In the new designs hard corners were gradually rounded off, a hint of the waist appeared and coats flared more gracefully. Yet when Dior's New Look burst upon the scene in 1947 the public was not ready for it and could not stifle a chorus of disapproval. Cloth-counting had gained such a grip on women that they were stunned by the thought of the thirty to forty yards required for the new fashions. The fact that they also required luxury corsets (or "hipettes"), advertised at 25/6 (£1.28 $5.12) a pair, seemed the height of bad taste.

At first the New Look had very little impact on the housewives of France and Britain. One of the first of the new dresses was torn off the back of a model girl in the rue Lepic, while women screamed "40,000 francs for a dress and our children have no milk!" In North America (outside New York) disapproval was so strong that when Dior toured the States in 1947 he was met in Chicago by mobs of females with posters saying "Burn Mr Dior", "Christian Dior Go Home". In Dallas, Texas, where he went to receive an Oscar, 1,300 women joined the Little Below the Knee Club to protest against the new length. Within a year the *volte-face* was complete and the New Look, shorn of its Rue de la Paix extravagances, was seen everywhere. But how it looked, and how it began, belong to another chapter.

The uniforms of an RAF flight lieutenant and an army tank corps captain./*Tailor and Cutter*

WRNS uniform, showing the correct angle at which the new hat of 1942 was to be worn./ *Imperial War Museum*

The basic pattern of dress of all the services and auxiliary services came into use in *1936-7*, though when the Second World War broke out many enlisters were forced to wear First World War uniforms. The war carried the forces into new tests and research to produce clothing to withstand unusual conditions of wear and weather. Standard fabrics for the ranks were woollen serge and officers wore barathea, cavalry twill or gabardine, depending on how much they could afford to spend. By *1940* there were *1,000* khaki manufacturers in Britain (there had been nine before the war) turning out a total of *150,000* yards per month.

MAKE-DO AND MEND

says Mrs. Sew-and-Sew

Dungarees and pinafore dresses were very popular with the working woman. They were often made of durable fabrics such as linen, sailcloth and dyed calico. Basically they were overalls, worn to save other garments from everday wear, but as a style dungarees even crept up into the *haute couture* bracket, appearing in Piguet's 1942 collection./*D. H. Evans 1940 and Radio Times Hulton Picture Library 1941*

Top right:
Poster issued by the Board of Trade to encourage economy in the home./*Imperial War Museum*

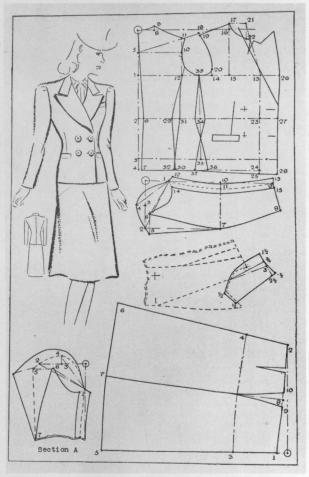

Above:
The "utility" scheme began in Britain in 1941, the emphasis being on saving fabric by economical design and on eliminating labour-consuming detail from dress. In 1941 the *Tailor and Cutter* showed how pattern pieces could be laid out to save cloth./*Tailor and Cutter*

In 1942 London's leading designers formed the Incorporated Society of London Fashion Designers, one of their tasks being to design utility wear that was both attractive and inexpensive. The original eight members were Angèle Delange, Norman Hartnell, Bianca Mosca, Digby Morton, Peter Russell, Victor Stiebel, Worth of London and their chairman, Edward Molyneux. Hartnell was associated with the manufacturing firm of Berketex and designed these dresses for them. Both were made from Scottish wools./ *Keystone Press Agency*

Wartime clothing regulations allowed for little variation or originality and the differences between cheap and expensive suits were minimal, usually lying only in the quality of the cloth. The picture illustrates this with a model suit (*left*) and its mass-produced counterpart (*right*) made in 1942./*Keystone Press Agency*

A typical outfit for 1943 – black
and white striped suit, a small
green felt hat with matching
scarf and gloves, plaited straw
shoulder bag and black cuban
heeled shoes./*Moss Bros*

Above:
After the war women who had
worn service dress for the
duration were encouraged to
revive their interest in fashion.
Here a mannequin displays a
demob costume to an audience
of servicewomen. The total
cost of the outfit was £12.50
($50.00)./*Keystone Press Agency*

14

Above left:
A simple cavalier cape of 1944, with stand-up collar. Few wartime coats had buttons – which were strictly rationed – so most coats were simply wrapped round the body./ *Bradleys*

Above right/below:
Spring suits and summer frocks for 1945. The postwar severity is relieved by pleats, tucks, piping and pockets with decorated flaps – details that were forbidden a year earlier when rationing was at its height./*Marshall and Snelgrove*

PRACTICAL CHRISTMAS PRESENTS

1 **S**lightly Fleeced Hood. In leaf green, mermaid, wine, saxe, navy, dark cherry, royal, emerald, rust and tan.   **6/6**
(No coupons)

2 **L**arge Hand Crochet Beret in large range of shades, including royal, black, wine, parma violet, cherry, brown, navy, emerald, bottle, grey, scarlet, tan. With quill.
(No coupons)   **23/3**
Without quill, 21/9

3 Child's Woollen Jersey, with collar. In moon blue, almond green and scarlet. Size 28 in.   **9/4**
(4 coupons)
Sizes 30 in., **10/2**; 32 in., **11/-** (4 coupons)
Fair Isle Berets, from **22/6**

4 Boy's Cable Stitch Slipover, in dark grey. Size 26 in.   **13/2**
(4 coupons)
Sizes 28 in., **13/6**; 30 in., **13/11**; 32 in., **14/3** (4 coupons)

Children's Knitwear — Second Floor

5 An **Example** from our stock of Cardigan Suits for young ladies. The style sketched is in green, scarlet, wine. Hip sizes 38 and 40 in. (For *personal shoppers only.*)   **51/11**
(12 coupons)

Hand crochet chenille Hat with peak, as sketch, in tan, green, blue, brown, black, grey, 30/9 (no coupons)

6 Child's Breechette Set, with Hood or Beret, in fine knitted wool. Shades : Saxe blue, green and cherry. Coat length 14 in. **19/-** (5 coupons)
Coat length 16 in., **20/8**
Other styles and colours at proportionate prices.

Page Eighteen

Knitwear and coat for the under-fives (1945)./*Marshall and Snelgrove*

Childrens' clothes could be made out of odds and ends such as cotton sheets, discarded adult dresses, tablecloths or old black-out curtains, and magazines were full of advice on how to enlarge an outgrown garment. Clothes that were bought new had to be functional and hardwearing.

A typical romantic studio photograph of children dressed for a wedding or special occasion. Photographers were still taking portrait pictures against painted backcloths and the group shows marked Victorian traces, the impression conveyed being that children should be seen and not heard./ *Cotton Board*

The
drawings
by
Louise Ambler

pinafore

Ideas for making pinafore
frocks (1945)./*Harper's Bazaar*

● For those who are short of coupons and whose children have grown out of last year's frocks, we here present the new-old idea of pinafores. Worn either protectively over a " best " dress or as a cover-up over a shabby one, they are practical, attractive and beautifully easy to make. Any of the eight variations of the pinafore theme sketched here could be made from an odd length of material or even from a scarf.

1 and 2. Cut up the skirt of a grown-up cotton frock or chop the end off a chintz or cretonne curtain to make either of these two, both perfect for romping in the nursery or garden.

3. One white linen or cotton sheet would make at least two of this combination of romper-suit and pinafore, bound and embellished with any bright material you have handy.

4. Hunt out those discarded blackout curtains for this pinafore, like those that French children wear, ideal for getting inky in the schoolroom and for " grubbing " in the garden.

5. If you have Scotch blood and your own tartan kilt, or an old dress of tartan material, consider cutting it up to make this gay pleated pinafore with a cosy pair of " trews " to match.

6. Sacrifice a linen tea-cloth, and hunt up some narrow bits of lace to edge the ruffles of this fresh-as-a-daisy, party-pretty pinafore like Alice wore when she went to Wonderland.

7. Put your own, or your husband's, khaki uniform to good new use by converting it into a different sort of battle-dress, the perfect pinafore for a tom-boy ; match it with a khaki jersey.

8. Convert a cotton table-cloth, or a couple of scarves, into this ruffled pinafore of sense and sensibility.

plan

7

6

5

8

EXAMPLES of the SALE OFFERS

DEBUTANTES

Summer Spot Dress in rayon that looks like linen. In blue, green, pink and stone. Original price £5.9.9

Sale price 50/-
(7 coupons)

Debutante Frocks Second Floor

EXTRA-SIZE GOWNS

Oddments in large size Gowns, in hip fittings 44, 46 and 48 in. Many at less than half-price. Example sketched. Original price £10.6.0.

Sale price £4
(7 coupons)

Extra-size Gowns First Floor

INEXPENSIVE GOWNS

Special reduction in lovely Summer Jumper Suits in a novelty material. Several colours. Original price £9.4.10.

Sale price £4
(10 coupons)

Inexpensive Gowns First Floor

Have Lunch or Tea in the Restaurant—3rd Floor

SALE BEGINS JULY 15

SKIRTS

A group of good quality well tailored Tweed Skirts, at greatly reduced prices. Sketched is an example.

Sale price 50/-
(6 coupons)

Skirts Ground Floor

COATS

Oddments in well tailored Coats in good materials, including tweeds. Typical example sketched. Original prices 15 gns. to £20.

Sale price £10
(18 coupons)

Coats Ground Floor

EXTRA SIZE GOWNS

Lovely black and white over-check Suits. Sizes 44 and 46 in. Original price £11.9.1.

Sale price £10
(10 coupons)

Frocks, in the same material. Original price £8.12.8.

Sale price £8
(7 coupons)

Extra-size Gowns First Floor

Marshall & Snelgrove, Oxford Street, London, W.1

20

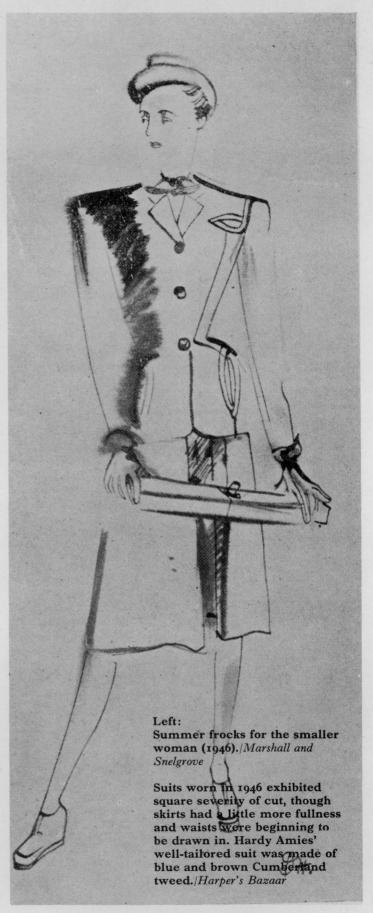

Left:
Summer frocks for the smaller woman (1946)./*Marshall and Snelgrove*

Suits worn in 1946 exhibited square severity of cut, though skirts had a little more fullness and waists were beginning to be drawn in. Hardy Amies' well-tailored suit was made of blue and brown Cumberland tweed./*Harper's Bazaar*

The New Look erupted in Paris in 1947, giving a softer, more rounded line to the silhouette. The dress and suit in the pictures show the new mid-calf length of 1948, the pulled-in waist and the naturally rounded shoulders that characterized the look. Pleats gave an extra fullness to the skirt, though the excesses of Paris models were avoided. Slim-line skirts, which appeared in all collections, were also longer and were often complemented by an umbrella carried to emphasize the line./*The John French Photo Library*

21

Left:
Civilian wear for men during the war ran along traditional lines and has hardly varied since. This coat, drawn in 1940, is almost dateless./*Tailor and Cutter*

Right:
Suits in the war years were commonly double-breasted and trousers had turn-ups; waistcoats were discouraged because of the shortage of cloth but Savile Row tailors were anxious to retain their popularity, justifying them on the grounds of warmth. Colours were restrained: the suit in the picture is made of grey flannel with white pinstripes (1941)./*Tailor and Cutter*

Above:
A hasty deal in London's Oxford Street shows a woman inspecting a pair of much-coveted nylon stockings offered by street merchants in 1950./
Radio Times Hulton Picture Library

After the war servicemen were issued with a demob suit, a shirt, two collars, two pairs of socks, one pair of shoes, a pair of cufflinks, a tie and a hat, to celebrate their return to normal life. The choice was limited and suits were hurriedly made, often in inferior fabrics. The illustration shows a fitting in 1946./*Radio Times Hulton Picture Library*

Left:
Postwar menswear was inspired
by service uniforms, as this
tweed jacket, sponsored by the
Board of Trade in 1947
indicates. The tie belt is
reminiscent of the battledress
jacket./*Radio Times Hulton
Picture Library*

Arms and the man present no terrors to our students once they
have taken their third degree at our Academy of Salesmanship.

Hire firms such as Moss Bros
thrived in the postwar period,
as many people whose
wardrobes had been depleted
by austerity were forced to hire
clothes for one-off special
occasions. The cartoonist
William Heath Robinson poked
fun in a series of cartoons
which Moss Bros handed out
to their customers./*Moss Bros*

A mass-production copy of Dior's New Look incorporating all the features of the 1947 fashion: long full skirt, slender waist, low-cut neck, black gloves, capped by a boat-shaped hat./*Catriona Tomalin*

Paris Fashion

Europe and America may have been slow to react to the New Look but Paris immediately recognized it as the vitalizing force needed to revive the reputation of *haute couture*.

The industry had come near to total collapse during the Occupation and it was thanks to the diplomatic dealings of Lucien Lelong, who managed to walk a tightrope over the heads of the Germans for four years, that couture survived in Paris. When the Germans arrived in 1940 they broke into the offices of the Chambre Syndicale de la Couture Parisienne and seized all documents relating to the French fashion export trade and schools of dressmaking. Their idea was to shift the industry to Vienna and Berlin, where they could gain tighter control over it, but Lelong managed to persuade them that such a move would kill the industry dead. Paris had been regarded as the centre for chic ever since the sixteenth century, when France's supremacy in silk and lace making was undisputed, and from that time onwards a system of complementary industries essential to the fashion trade had been built up. To separate Paris and fashion would have been like removing the heart from its fine web of interacting veins and arteries. Besides this, it would have been fatal to remove the designers from the milieu of elegance from which they drew their inspiration. By repeated discussions (fourteen conferences in four years) Lelong managed to keep open ninety-two houses (though only the top twelve had privileges) and 112,000 skilled workers were saved from compulsory labour in German war industries. Paris retained its traditional position as the centre of the fashion trade, while Germany failed to produce a single designer of note.

German women in Paris were known as *souris grises* (grey mice), presumably because they dressed in drab grey, so it naturally became the ambition of every Parisienne to wear clothes contrasting as sharply as possible with the alien influence. The couture houses accordingly produced a series of outlandish styles that showed little concern for wartime restrictions. Hats in particular fired the imagination of designers, blooming in a riot of stupendous concoctions of flowers, beads, ribbons, feathers and even newspaper and wood-shavings. The French millinery industry enlisted the support of the fashion model Bettina to uphold the popularity of the hat, making her promise never to be seen in the streets or in restaurants without one. She lived up to her word, only to be humiliated one evening at Maxim's by being cut dead by a Mr André Dubonnet, who explained next day that he felt ashamed to acknowledge one whose *Vogue*-like appearance seemed so inappropriate to the time. Nevertheless the bright scarlet bonnet she flaunted on that occasion must have brightened the otherwise depressed city.

After the Liberation the Chambre Syndicale rallied, to prove that couture had survived in full force. They now created the *Théâtre de la Mode* – a collection of dolls dressed in the latest silhouettes which went on a tour of all the major European and North American cities. All the leading designers took part in the display, collaborating to revive the dying cocktail dress. Typical examples had short, wide skirts, and décolleté bodices covered (at least for the first part of the evening) with a bolero.

In 1945 collections revealed a definite trend towards the femininity women had so long been denied. Padding came out of the shoulders and a natural rounded line was stressed. V-neck sweaters hinted at décolletage. Pockets, revers, buttons, feathers and ribbons burst back into fashion with all the acclaim of something long awaited; pockets were everywhere, buttons grew as big as saucers. In the following year the House of Lelong (Dior was one of their designers) heralded the approaching change with the "Winterhalter skirt" of candy pink tulle sprinkled with feathers. This ultra-feminine style reminded people of the Empress Eugénie, one of the most influential patrons of French couture in the 1850s. Other collections showed lines that looked like closed umbrellas compared to Lelong's open parasol, their distinguishing feature being at the back, where bustle-like folds of fabric made women look as if they were walking against the wind, as indeed they were.

The New Look swept all before it, changing the silhouette completely. This is one of the rare occasions in fashion history when a change in style can be precisely dated, originating as it did on the day of Christina Dior's first collection, February 12th, 1947. Dior himself was not so arrogant as to call it a new look – the phrase was in fact coined by *Life* magazine – to him it was the "Corolle Line", first of many "lines". What enchanted fashion editors at the first viewing was the sense of luxury and soft femininity embodied in each dress, reminding them of how long they had been starved of such things. Yet it was not really a new look at all, for the nipped-in waists, padded hips and crinoline-swirling skirts dated back to the nineteenth century, and to the eighteenth and sixteenth centuries before that. But after seven years of utility wear it seemed like a breath of fresh air. Dior's shapely skirts, flowing to mid calf with the familiar motif of a miriad of hand-pressed pleats brought sculpture back into fashion, moulding drapery round the figure and highlighting the body's natural curves. Every model gown had to have a tight fitting corset built into it, and this was often "sculpted" into the required shape with a hot iron and the deft use of a new top-secret substance – paper-stiff nylon. The whole formed a sort of scaffolding that could all but stand up by itself. The dress was protected from the framework, as Mme Marguerite Carré, Dior's *première*, (or lieutenant) explained: first there was "the famous no. 132 tulle from Brivet, then a very sheer organza from Abraham. To prevent the tulle from scratching and making ladders in stockings, a very fine silk *pongé* was added to line the skirt."

Each design was the subject of much discussion, from the *première* who interpreted the designer's ideas and attended to every detail of its construction down to the sewing hands, who might spend anything from seventy to three hundred hours making up a complete outfit. Dior's ensembles offered a total look, with each detail thought out – shoes matching the dress, the bag, the hat, even the perfume were carefully planned to set off the wearer and her gown. Dior himself paid great attention to hats, for even though he admitted that they need not always be worn, he felt strongly that their shape and volume should balance the overall silhouette. His first hats were large, boat-like extravaganzas, but as skirts swirled to greater fullness and coats grew bulkier, so hats became neater and smaller. Dior now began to show tiny berets or toques, which were usually clapped to the side of the head and held in place with hatpins. The small hat focused attention on the neckline. This was either cut very wide and deep for cocktail and evening wear or rose excitingly high, embellished with a large stand-up collar reminiscent of the ruff.

By 1949 the New Look had fined down. The length crystallized into eleven inches from the ground for formal wear, rising to fourteen inches for country clothes. Waists were still tiny and made even more so by "waspie" corsets, coloured cummerbunds, leather and braided belts. The hips were still emphasised but less by padding than by effective cutting and odd gimmicks such as flared peplums to the jacket, jutting or double flap pockets, side pleats and stiff petticoats. Pleats soared into high fashion, appearing both on the skirt and on the jacket, running horizontally, vertically or sometimes diagonally.

Each year a new theme informed the latest Dior collection. In 1951, for instance, his designs were based on the princess line. In 1954, in deference to the threat of the H bomb, he launched the H line, which Carmel Snow (editor of *Harper's Bazaar*) named the "flat look", as it seemed to hint at a return to the flat-chested fashions of the twenties. This was followed in 1955 by the A and Y lines, the letters indicating the dominant shape. He justified his fluctuation by saying; "The feminine silhouette changes from season to season, just like our habits and thoughts. Women dress for fun, not just to cover themselves." Nevertheless it is important to remember that while Dior felt that he had to offer his metropolitan clients something new every year, it took many years for one of his fashions to die out in the country and the provinces. Most women could not afford to jettison their whole wardrobe every time a new style was "in". In 1956 Dior launched the first of his popular tunic dresses, followed in 1957 by the Free Line. This year also saw the introduction of a fitted wool chemise dress in a small herringbone pattern, with a crew neck and long sleeves. This heralded the loose shapes developed by Dior's protégé Yves Saint Laurent in his Trapeze line of 1958, the year when he designed his first collection for the house of Dior after its founder's sudden death.

The proper author of the loosely hanging chemise dress was in fact the Spanish-born couturier Cristobal Balenciaga, who, with Dior, was the most influential designer of the fifties. In 1954 he was showing loose tunic tops to be worn over long slim skirts and in 1957 he introduced the perfectly straight, unfitted "chemmy dress", narrowing at the hem, that became known as the sack dress. Its popularity was due to the strange idea that emancipated woman cannot have her waist in the right place, since this would indicate (or necessitate) tight corseting.

Balenciaga shortened the sleeves to a pretty three-quarter length to balance the looseness over the hips. His sack dresses were wildly popular, although in spite of their simplicity of cut they were very expensive. Particularly treasured were his evening gowns which displayed yards and yards of silk. He was the only one of the Paris designers to bring the influence of his own country to the clothes he made, with the result that his shapes are often described as "pure Goya". He was also one of the few designers who was familiar with all the intricacies of cutting, sewing and fitting every part of a garment himself (Charles James in the United States was another), for most couturiers relied on their *premières* to interpret their ideas for them. He also opted out of the regulations for showing collections imposed by the Chambre Syndicale who arranged the times of press showings during "The Week" so that no two collections could be viewed at the same time. In fact he put every difficulty in the path of buyers, forcing them to come back to Paris solely to see his show, which took place weeks after all the others, and insisting on an exceptionally high deposit of £1,000 ($2,800), without which no buyer was allowed to enter his sanctuary. He avoided publicity, never gave interviews and did not market any of the fringe attractions such as stockings, shoes or scarves with which couture houses tempted the less wealthy who still wanted something with a couture label. He was a perfectionist and was highly selective not only in the fabric for his clothes but also in the women he was willing to dress. So it is not surprising that, expensive as they were, every chic woman longed to own one of his creations. Indeed they were so highly prized and so frequently worn that very few remain in a wearable state today. His decision to retire from couture in 1968 was caused by his realisation that the era of aristocratic elegance was finally over and that youth and vitality were becoming the basis of all couture.

Jacques Fath was one of the first designers to emerge as a champion of younger colours, using blue and green together at a time when only black and brown ranked as chic. But colour was his only concession to youth. In 1948 he created as great a sensation as Dior's New Look with his crippling hobble skirts, which were so long and so tight that his mannequins could hardly walk in them. They certainly did not represent fashion for the masses, as *Picture Post* pointed out: "Can anyone seriously contemplate hopping on a bus in a hobble skirt?" And yet thousands of women attempted to do just that, in imitation of the slim line that delighted Fath and looked so glamorous on model girls and air hostesses. Pencil-slim skirts remained high fashion throughout the fifties, variations occurring only in the length and style of the vent or slit at the back to allow room for movement.

Among Paris designers, only Gabrielle Chanel thought freedom of movement more important than the overall silhouette. She reopened her fashion house in 1954 after a gap of fourteen years. What is so extraordinary about Chanel's reappearance is that when she returned she showed almost exactly the same styles as she had in the twenties and thirties – easy-fitting suits, with collarless cardigan jackets, pretty pastel-coloured blouses with "pussy-cat" bows and the little black dress that appeared in every collection. She staged her comeback at exactly the right moment, when people had still not shaken off the after-effects of war. Now her soft, natural lines made them realise how austere and forced the silhouette had become. By the end of the fifties "Chanel suits" were seen everywhere and it gave her immense pleasure to see how strongly she had influenced the way women dressed. Other fashions developed alongside hers, but when in doubt women could always fall back on the timeless safety of a Chanel. The colours and fabrics were the only things that changed from year to year, yet in certain élite circles great importance was attached to the wearing of a new Chanel direct from the couturière herself, for nowhere else could one obtain the same perfection of fit. Chanel's brand of perfectionism is well illustrated in a remark she is alleged to have made to an American model: "Certain women wear a suit; certain suits wear women. In the first case the woman is bad; in the second the suit is not good."

No doubt Chanel viewed with some distaste the extravagances of her compatriot Givenchy, who in 1957 launched the puff-ball silhouette (borrowed from the Italian designer Capucci). This was a curious distortion of the body's shape, combining the sack dress with the popular crinoline skirts stiffened with a paper petticoat initiated by Dior. The puff-ball skirt was bell-shaped and was gathered into a narrow hem, its *bouffant* outline balanced by stark simplicity in the bodice which was frequently strapless. A later version was the barrel skirt, with a wide band at the waist matched by a similar band at the hem. These skirts were so difficult to iron that they died a natural death after two or three years, for by that time the sixties were approaching and with them came young and carefree clothing and a new approach to couture.

For decades the world of haute couture had depended on the strictly organized hierarchy of the Paris fashion house. This structure had scarcely varied since the days of the first Worth, who had designed the Empress Eugénie's wonderful *ensembles* in the 1850s and initiated many of the traditions of French couture.

The head of the whole team was the designer, who worked in strictest secrecy and divulged his ideas only to his *première*, who is in fact not necessarily a woman, as the feminine title seems to suggest. Some designers – Dior is one example – produced as many as 600 or 700 sketches, which were discussed in detail with the *première*. The total was fined down to about 100 and these then went forward for the collection proper. Others, such as Fath and Grès worked directly with the fabric, draping it over a dummy or a living model and allowing its inherent qualities to suggest a design. Once the idea had been born, they took an inferior fabric, such as muslin, cutting and draping this until they could explain to their *première* exactly what effect they wanted to create. The *première* was then responsible for working out all the technical details and the design was made up in a cheaper fabric, which was used as a pattern for cutting out the final model. This top-secret process occurred entirely behind closed doors – especially if the designer felt confident that he had invented a new line – and the garment was not made up until the last moment, with several sewing hands working on it simultaneously but separately, so that none knew the final effect and therefore could not betray it. Secrecy was most strict at houses that were expected to be the season's trendsetters – usually only two or three houses competed for this privileged status each year.

The couturier had various personal assistants besides his *première*. His fabric specialists, for instance, could tell him in which direction a material could or could not be cut, while a couple of sketchers were available to put the ideas down on paper. Other essential roles were played by the business manager, the press officer and the *directrice*, who oversaw all the *vendeuses*. The *vendeuse* represented the link between the client and the rest of the couture trade. Although essentially a glorified saleslady, she was usually very grand and very chic and she personally supervised all the details of the client's order. It was she who took the store buyer's deposit, which ranged at that time from £100 to £500 ($280 and $1,400) or in exceptional cases even more. This deposit was non-returnable, but it did go towards the price of the models ordered, each of which might cost anything from £250 to £1,000 ($700 to $2,800). Often the price was not calculated until after the show, for only then could the number of hours of work involved be assessed. For complicated gowns hundreds of hours might be spent by sewing hands in the workrooms attached to the couture house. These were usually tiny basements where seamstresses inevitably ruined their eyesight, yet hard as the work was, there was fierce competition for a place in a fashion house and every girl who started by picking up pins hoped to be at the head of her studio one day. Lelong estimated that it took as long as seven years to train an expert sewing hand.

When one considers how much training and effort went into the creation of a single Paris gown, its high expense seems justifiable – in these terms alone. But it was all part of the mystique of *haute couture* and the exclusive, elegant world of high society, a world that was fast vanishing. The rigid hierarchy of the Paris fashion house had been a necessary auxiliary of this old order but this had been profoundly disturbed by the democratizing effects of the world war. Paris fashion houses still exist today and have the same structure but they have been profoundly disturbed by mass-culture and mass-production.

In the forties *haute couture* still depended on the old social élite, a world peopled by extravagantly rich women such as the American Mrs Biddle, who would arrive with her jewelry casket and order her dresses to match the colour of her gems, or the Spanish Mme Anchorena, who ordered 28 million francs worth of dresses per year, often choosing the same model in different shades, as well as fur coats and hats to complete the ensemble. But as the forties ended and the fifties began, such ostentatiously wealthy clients began to disappear. As the new decade progressed the number of private customers willing or able to pay for individuality was continually dwindling. Mass-production now began to be the basis for the fashion trade, with store buyers and manufacturers ordering several models from the Paris houses with a licence to mass-produce them in their own countries. American buyers were the most popular because they had the three F's – Faith, Figures and Francs. Buyers for big American stores such as Bonwit Teller or Lord and Taylor were treated like mini filmstars: cars and boxes at the opera were put at their disposal, flowers filled their rooms and accessory salesmen presented them with lavish gifts. The trade was of great importance to France, bringing the country an average income of £100 million ($280m), and the biannual collections were headline news, generating such excitement during "The Week" (more often than not a fortnight) that even the taxi drivers would know the times and details of the important shows.

There were, and still are, three ways in which a buyer could obtain a model for mass-production. She could buy a prototype exactly as seen in the collection, but she paid more than a private client because she was entitled to unpick it and use it as a pattern. Alternatively, and at a more favourable price, she could buy a *toile*, which was the model made up in *toile de coton*, unlined but with the details sketched in. The third and least expensive alternative was to buy a paper pattern with a sketch of the original material attached, but it was understood that she would never sell the pattern or make a modified version of it and that the manufactured garment was to have a strictly limited run. A large chain of stores would often have only two or three of the same dress on the racks in any one town, so guaranteeing its clientele a more or less exclusive look – a privilege that was naturally reflected in the price. The store was also expected to display the name of the originating house. On the face of it, it looks as if it would be easy enough for copyists to poach ideas without buying a model, but the Chambre Syndicale has always maintained a very efficient legal department to check on possible infringement of copyright ideas, and in their heyday the large couture houses would expect to have two or three lawsuits on their hands at any one time.

The couture houses were slow to recognize the need to design directly for mass-production and Jacques Heim, who noted the wind of change as early as 1950, had to keep his dealings with a manufacturer a closely guarded secret, lest his colleagues should think he was bastardizing the trade. By the end of the fifties, however, most designers had a ready-to-wear boutique attached to their houses and most of their revenue depended on them. Only the uncompromising Balenciaga held out against what he considered to be an adulteration of the purity of Paris couture. His departure from the world of *haute couture* in 1968 marked the end of an era in the history of fashion. He closed his house because he saw that couture could no longer compete with mass-production and he did not want to join with it. In a sense the fifties was the last fling of Paris couture.

By 1946 Paris had re-established herself as the fashion centre of the world. The spring collections showed floating skirts, flowers tucked into the bosom, décolleté evening gowns and short, full cocktail frocks./*Harper's Bazaar*

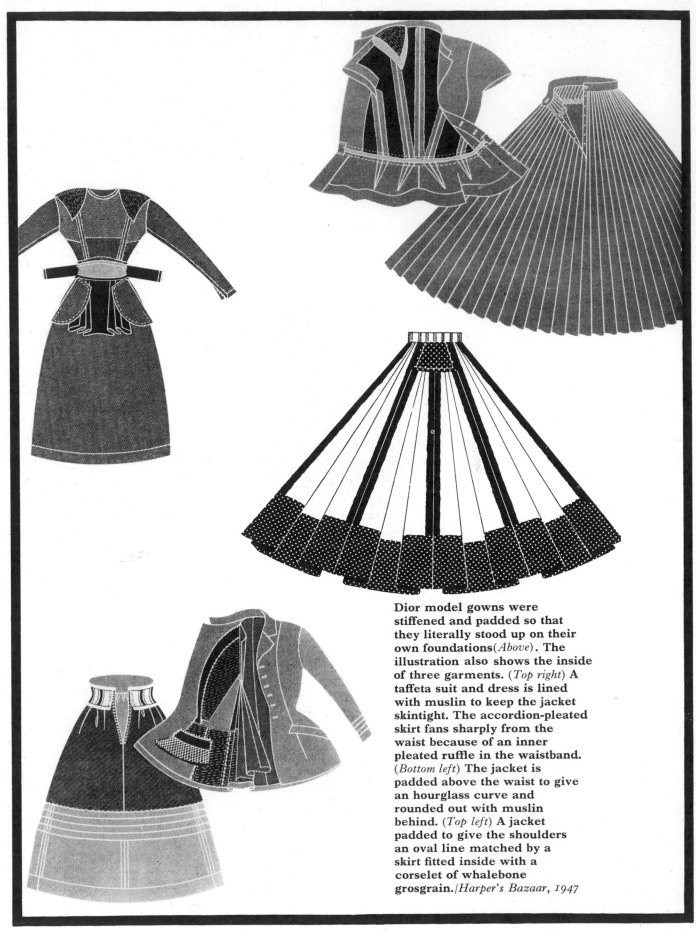

Dior model gowns were stiffened and padded so that they literally stood up on their own foundations(*Above*). The illustration also shows the inside of three garments. (*Top right*) A taffeta suit and dress is lined with muslin to keep the jacket skintight. The accordion-pleated skirt fans sharply from the waist because of an inner pleated ruffle in the waistband. (*Bottom left*) The jacket is padded above the waist to give an hourglass curve and rounded out with muslin behind. (*Top left*) A jacket padded to give the shoulders an oval line matched by a skirt fitted inside with a corselet of whalebone grosgrain./*Harper's Bazaar, 1947*

The 1948 line was a toned-down version of the New Look. Waists were pulled in and tightly belted, sleeves were three-quarter length and dresses featured decoration on the corsage, such as the vast bow on Dior's dress (*Above*) and the rose on Piguet's polka dot dress (*right*)./*Harper's Bazaar*

Left:
Dior's alternative featured narrow barrel skirts with hipbone pleats. The picture shows a cutaway jacket and lengthened skirt from his second collection in 1947./*Maison Dior*

Above:
Jacques Fath was famous for his slender line. He had a strong feeling for angles and points, exploiting the potential of collars, cuffs and short capes. This black suit was shown in his autumn 1949 collection./ *Harper's Bazaar*

The 1952 Paris collections made much of extra-large buttons. In the picture a jut-out collar from a Schiaparelli coat (*top*) and a Dessès coat with button-up front neckline on a cracker-shaped coat (*below*) feature button detail. Paris favoured a domed look, with bulk at the top of the silhouette./*Harper's Bazaar*

Paris's top model Bettina came to Britain to promote French chic. Here she is seen (*left*) in 1951 in a Brenner Sports coat and (*right*) trying on an ordinary man's shirt bought from a chain store for this appealing picture taken in 1952./*The John French Photo Library and Radio Times Hulton Picture Library*

The pre-collection line for
1952, which was almost
identical to what had been
shown in Paris a couple of
years previously, showing how
this type of silhouette
persisted./*The John French Photo
Library*

Right:
This cotton dress by Dior
created a stir when it appeared
in his 1952 spring collection.
Hitherto cotton had been
regarded as a distinctly plebian
fabric unsuitable for evening
wear but Ascher's printed
cotton designed by a well-
known artist of the time
brought this neglected fabric
into evening wear./*Mr Z. Ascher*

The influence of fabric design on couture has often been underrated, as fashion writers tend to look at the shape of the silhouette rather than at its component materials. One of the major fashion revolutions of the fifties was the increasing popularity of flowered fabrics for dresses, a revolution initiated by Ascher of London. Dior was the first designer to make use of Ascher's designs, one of the most successful being the rose pompom dress of 1954 (*middle*), which ran into several editions. Later came stylized flowers of 1955 (*left*) and the beautiful silk evening dress of 1956 (*right*) which introduced subtle prints in colour on colour. Dior commented, "Fabric not only expresses a designer's dreams but also stimulates his own ideas. It can be the beginning of an inspiration. Many a dress of mine is born of the fabric alone."/Mr Z. Ascher

40

Far left:
A contrast to Dior's flared line is shown in Givenchy's 1954 silhouette which, in fashion magazine terminology, "stresses the isthmus cartography of the body". The drawing shows a narrow black suit, precisely waisted, almost sleeveless, muffled in a towering white organdie scarf pierced with a sheaf of satin hyacinths./*Harper's Bazaar*

Middle:
A new fabric mixture of silk, wool and Acrilan inspired Balmain to make this pink suit and jacket in 1955. The fabric is made by the British firm of Sekers, who specialized in synthetic mixtures. A quota restriction in the use of British fabrics by French fashion houses led to fierce competition between British manufacturers to have their products accepted by the top Paris houses./*Radio Times Hulton Picture Library*

Left:
Leading model Anne Gunning wears a Dior A line suit (1955). The photograph neatly shows why it was named after the first letter of the alphabet./ *The John French Photo Library*

Dark in the evening

4. LANVIN-CASTILLO. Theatre coat stopping short at the ankles—new length for after six. The coat, black velvet and moiré, the lining, white satin like the whiplash dress beneath (Hurel fabrics). A white evening hat like a motoring cap.

5. GIVENCHY. Settecento evening wrap, a great pyramid of opaque, heavy black satin cuir (fabric by Abraham) envelops a pale pink satin dress.

6. GIVENCHY. Short strapless evening dress with his insistent backward thrust, the fullness held with buttoned bands. The fabrics, black embossed velvet and satin by Bianchini. A single full-blown rose covers the chignon at the back of the head.

7. GIVENCHY. Black again—the mood is sombre: a velvet dress divided down the front by a wide span of moiré continued in a halter neck.

8. LANVIN-CASTILLO. *Variation espagnole:* a ruffed Spanish cape of El Greco brown satin, over a narrow dress of the same fabric (by Hurel). The jewellery, dull black beads like rosary beads.

Left:
The 1955 line featured an
inverted Y, achieved by the use
of flying panels, flowing skirts
and roomy capes. In the picture
are evening designs by
Givenchy and Lanvin-Castillo./
Harper's Bazaar

An evening dress by Jean
Dessès (1956) in satin organza
shaped to look like rose petals,
interwoven to give a delicate
play of light and shade./*Mr Z.
Ascher*

Left:
The mohair and cotton mixture
from which this coat was made
created a sensation when it
appeared in Lanvin-Castillo's
collection for 1957. The fabric
was soft and light and
strengthened to prevent
sagging. It was made by
Ascher, who gave Lanvin-
Castillo exclusivity for a season.
The first six coats were so
successful that no less than
seventy-two repeats of one
model sold in the first week.
Mohair was one of the most
outstanding novelties of the
fifties and became very
fashionable./Mr Z. Ascher

Two dresses by different
couturiers designed in the
same fabric, again by Ascher.
It is printed silk dupion with
red flowers on a paler red
background. Balenciaga (left)
used it to make one of his first
sack dresses – the straightening
of the line is already clear –
while Lanvin-Castillo (right)
created a simple dress with
jacket. From the 1957
collections./Mr Z. Ascher

44

Left /Above:
Paris fashions were copied all
over the world. On this page is
a version of Givenchy's puff-ball
silhouette, followed by the
barrel-shaped line. The dress
on the left is by Lore Krampf of
Germany, and was made up
by Christian Dior. The cocktail
dress is by Sif Olsson of
Sweden. Both are 1957
creations./*International Wool
Secretariat*

Above right:
A wedding dress from Yves
Saint Laurent's first collection
for the House of Dior, showing
the trapeze line, which was a
voluminous version of the
sack./*Maison Dior*

47

Alix Grès was a designer who went her own way draping the fabric over the figure in soft Grecian folds. This evening gòwn was made in white silk jersey in 1959./*Camera Press*

Far right:
A mohair coat made in an azalea gold shade, designed for the busy career girl who never has time to take off her coat between calls. Designed by Guy Laroche in 1957, it is a typical version of the sack line./*Mr Z. Ascher*

Right:
Pierre Cardin was one of the first couturiers to predict the swing towards clothes designed in a younger image. In this 1958 outfit he put a youthful slant on the mohair fashion with his short top and lurex-threaded pants./*Mr Z. Ascher*

Top:
Cardin's spring fashions for 1959. The outfits feature the popular three-quarter length sleeves and the collarless jackets that were to become very common in the sixties, with stiletto heels and hats matching the silhouette. The backwards bend of the models is typical of Cardin, who tried to match his clothes to current styles in architecture./*Camera Press*

London's collections were sponsored by the Incorporated Society of London Fashion Designers and were timed to take place ten days before the Paris openings. An average of sixty models would be shown at each collection (compared with two hundred in Paris). In 1946, when this drawing was made, London's clothes were still largely for export only, though copies were appearing in some British stores. *Harper's Bazaar*

LONDON OPENINGS

Britain Can Make It

British historians are fond of giving names to decades, implying that everything happening in a ten-year span can be grouped under one heading. Often the division between one "age" and another is illusory, yet events in Britain were such that 1950 did indeed mark a dividing-line between the "age of austerity" and the "age of the affluent society". In this year the Labour government, whose stringent but inevitably unpopular measures had helped to set the country back on its feet, failed to obtain a workable majority in the House. In 1951 the Conservatives were voted back into power to enjoy a period of slow consolidation and increasing prosperity, to such an extent that Harold Macmillan felt himself entitled to use the celebrated slogan "You've Never Had It So Good" in his 1959 election campaign.

It was, however, under the Labour government that Britain celebrated her recent advances in the visual and decorative arts, fashion included, first in the "Britain Can Make It" Exhibition of 1946 and then in the 1951 Festival of Britain. The first exhibition was staged by the new Council for Industrial Design and was intended to boost Britain's export drive. The display occupied 90,000 square feet of the Victoria and Albert Museum, which was still empty as its treasures were in store, and was meant to "intensify the interest of manufacturers and distributors in industrial design, and their awareness of the desirability of rapid progress; to arouse greater interest in design in the minds of the general public . . . and to stage a prestige advertisement, before the world for British industry . . ." Clothing and accessories were naturally included, and indeed so much interest was focused on women's wear, which was displayed beneath a vast white canopy, that a separate catalogue was printed to itemize the garments shown. Dress fabrics were also included, draped across winged horses in flight and over the arms of tree women. The whole exhibition formed an excuse to produce luxury goods and lavish decoration of a kind that had not been seen at home for years. Thousands of colour-starved Britons lined up six deep round the Museum in their enthusiasm

to feast their eyes on the new materials that had come into existence since the war. Six thousand products were itemized, but almost everything was tantalizingly marked "For Export Only", so the public, while acclaiming its success, ruefully renamed the show "Britain Can't Have It".

Even so the exhibition did succeed in its main aim of giving Britain a therapeutic pat on the back, and people looked forward to a second morale-boosting display, which was planned to take place in 1951. Unlike its predecessor, the outward-looking Great Exhibition of 1851, which it was designed to commemorate, the Festival of Britain turned in on itself, aiming to show "the British contribution to civilization past, present, and future in the arts, sciences, and technology and in industrial design." It was to be a year of fun, fantasy and colour with open air cafés, striped umbrellas, fanciful buildings such as the Dome of Discovery and the Skylon. Everything was painted in strong primary colours that marked a premeditated departure from the stifling weight of Victorian grandeur and the beginning of a new, Scandinavian-inspired, style – Contemporary. A hundred or more designers were employed under the guidance of Herbert Morrison (Lord Festival!) and they co-operated with twenty-eight British manufacturers to ensure that everything down to the last litter bin and flower pot should conform to a total design concept. This overall concept was based in part on recent scientific discoveries and their translation into art forms, with the result that visitors saw products decorated with patterns derived from the structure of plastic, crystal-structure curtains, dress prints derived from haemoglobin and ties based on light waves. The display generated such enthusiasm that the journalist Marghanita Laski was to write in *The Observer* a year later, "It *was* nice wasn't it, last year, the Festival Year. It was the nicest thing that happened in England in the whole of my life."

Yet in spite of the feeling for a British style of design generated by the Festival, the fashion industry changed very little, hardly doing more than to combine "contemporary" dress fabrics with Paris-based designs. For it remained true throughout the forties and fifties that (as the *Sunday Times* remarked) "Paris makes fashion; London makes clothes".

During and after the war, London's "clothes" were divided into two groups. There were the high-fashion houses, which designed almost exclusively for export, and the mass-production stores and firms geared to supplying women's ordinary needs. British high fashion began to organize itself to meet export demands only after the collapse of Paris in 1940, which gave it the chance to corner the prosperous American market. In 1942 the Incorporated Society of London Fashion Designers was formed and its eight founder members (Norman Hartnell, Edward Molyneux, Angèle Delange, Digby Morton, Worth of London, Victor Stiebel, Bianca Mosca and Peter Russell) were granted special concessions throughout the period of rationing so that they could continue to design prestige-building garments. These acted as advertisements for British raw materials, such as English woollens and Scottish tweeds. The mainstay of the group during the war was Edward Molyneux, who brought his Paris house to London, thus giving other designers the benefit of his knowledge and exquisite taste.

After the war the London collections were shown one week before Paris, so there could be no question of copying, though London designs were decidedly imitative of basic Paris trends. They had, however, two advantages to attract buyers on their way to Paris. Firstly, London was not nearly so expensive – couture models could be bought for anything from £25 to £75 ($100 to $300) and the buyer's deposit, which was less than in Paris, was in the region of £50 ($200*). The second attraction was that Britain had the influence of royalty, for although there were no trendsetting dressers among the royal family, they did generate countless glittering occasions to inspire the talents of designers such as Norman Hartnell and Hardy Amies. Selections from the London collections were shown every season to a representative of royalty in settings of elegance that provided a splendid background for the clothes. After 1947 many gowns were orientated towards the débutante, since the ceremony of presentation to the monarch, suspended during the war years, was reinstated. Charity balls on a similar scale were held in the United States. These were immense undertakings requiring, on one typical occasion, a committee of 106 mothers and 142 débutantes, the eighteen year olds often wearing their first couture gown. Débutante gowns sometimes had to double up as wedding dresses. After all both were white and both involved stock designs in stock materials – brocades, tulles, lace and satin. Italianate neo-medieval gowns with high necklines, pointed bodices and tight sleeves

*Up to 1949.

predominated.

When the Queen, then Princess Elizabeth, married in 1947, her wedding dress conformed to the general pattern, with a distinct feeling of nostalgia for the Renaissance. But it was embroidered and decorated on a scale well beyond the reach of any but royalty. The designer, Norman Hartnell, found his inspiration in a Botticelli figure adorned in clinging ivory silk, with trails of jasmine, smilax, syringa and small white rose-like blossoms, and he translated these flowers into embroideries of white crystals and pearls. The difficulty of his task was increased by two restrictions – in the first place clothing was still rationed, and although the Princess was allowed 100 coupons, this had to cover a bridal train that stretched fourteen yards behind her; secondly, he had to ensure that the future Queen of England was not wearing anything that came from ex-enemy territory. The 10,000 tiny seed pearls with which the dress was oversewn were therefore ordered from the United States, and the Scottish firm of Wintherthur near Dunfermline, that had been commissioned to produce the satin, had to hunt round for silkworms that came neither from Italy nor from Japan. The final result was a dress of great beauty which soon recouped some of its cost as it went on show after the wedding (the proceeds were donated to charity). For the rest of her trousseau the princess ordered clothes inspired by the New Look, which helped considerably to make it a socially acceptable fashion in England.

Hartnell's second masterpiece for the Queen was her coronation robe of 1953. It was embroidered with the symbols of England, Scotland, Ireland and Wales – the rose, the thistle, the shamrock and the leek – each emblem appearing on the skirt in strict order of precedence. The lower half of the robe was embellished with the combined flowers of the Commonwealth countries assembled in a floral garland, each flower or leaf nestling round the motherly Tudor rose of England. The whole garment was bejewelled with amethysts, opals, topaz and rubies.

Hartnell's fame rests largely on the elaborately embroidered dresses he created for ceremonial occasions, but he also collaborated, mainly with the firm of Berketex, in making clothes for mass-production. He was indeed the first British couturier to enter the mass-market. In this, and also in his appointment as "Dressmaker to the Queen", he was followed by Hardy Amies, whose early successes were in meticulous tailoring. Trained at Lachasse, Amies opened his own house in 1946 and then in 1950 set up the first London "boutique", which sold sensible ready-to-wear suits, coats, dresses and cashmeres. By the end of the fifties, thirty-three British and Commonwealth firms were under licence to mass-produce Hardy Amies clothes for men and women. His most publicized association was with Hepworths in the sixties, though this venture in fact began tentatively as early as 1957, when he produced a range of men's shirts, ties, motoring coats and sports jackets, which appealed to men-about-town. The Amies influence on men's clothes even extended to shoes, knitwear and pyjamas. His skill lay in creating an image of the "total man" that was adopted all over the world – in the United States, Japan and New Zealand. His designs typified the ideal of the perfect English gentleman, based as they were on his view that clothes should either improve a man's figure or increase his status.

The fact that the ready-to-wear trade could now attract designers who worked "by appointment to royalty", indicated how much the industry had boomed since the war. "Ready-mades", far from being the shoddily made *confections* that in prewar days were regarded as beneath contempt, now began to compete with couture. Before the war there had virtually been only three off-the-peg manufacturers in Britain – Eastex, Matita and Dorville, and self-respecting firms such as Harrod's never left a maker's label inside the garment. By 1947, fourteen of the best wholesalers had banded together to form the Model House Group, which included twenty-seven manufacturers and twenty-seven associate members dealing with accessories. Highly professional shows were organized every year. Petrol rationing had made it impractical for the ordinary shopper to buy her clothes at the well-known London stores, so brand names started to appear on garments as a guarantee of quality. Names like Polly Peck, Horrocks, Linzi, London Town and Susan Small soon became household words. (It is interesting to note that the wheel has now turned full circle, with Susan Small designing the first royal "off-the-peg" wedding dress for Princess Anne in 1973.)

Ready-to-wear clothes were practical, if unadventurous. Their design was almost always modelled on Paris, but any idiosyncratic features would be removed so that a dress could run for up to five years on the racks without looking dated. The most successful British ready-to-wear firm of the fifties was Marks & Spencer, who did more than any other chainstore to bring details from the *haute couture* salons and boutiques of Paris and Rome to the high street. Their buyers spent thousands on model gowns, translating them for the masses into well-cut and well-made versions of the fashionable silhouette and incorporating recognizable details such as the Chanel cuff, a Balenciaga sleeve length, a Fontana collar or a Simonetta treatment of the yoke. And the final product was on sale for less than £5 ($12.80)! The price and quality were so favourable that limits had to be set on production to prevent suits, dresses and knitwear from becoming a national uniform. Marks & Spencer's profits more than quadrupled in the fifties, for there were few families in England who did not boast some of the firm's goods,

even if their only "M & S" garments were underwear, which had never before been so conveniently available, or children's clothes, which were cheap and colourful.

Marks & Spencer had their own design studio (which still exists), part of which concentrated on fabric design and research. They never repeated the same pattern two seasons running and always followed the latest trends. Fabrics of the forties and early fifties tended to be patterned with dots and dashes and vague scribbles, rather reminiscent of the abstract style of painting then in vogue. Marks & Spencer later had great success with the large floral prints initiated by Dior in 1954, but these eventually became associated with the cheap and vulgar. The fabric designers also kept abreast of the latest developments from the United States, who now led the field in textile research because Britain had failed to exploit her own early beginnings. Terylene, for instance, which was to revolutionize men's trousers, had been invented by John Whinfield at the research works of the British Calico Printer's Association in 1941, but the secret was sold to the United States for much-needed dollars, where the product became known as Dacron. By the mid-fifties, pleated skirts and trousers in Terylene were in every chainstore in Britain.

Alongside the development of artificial fibres, campaigns were organized to uphold the prestige of natural fibres. The International Wool Secretariat sponsored yearly fashion competitions to promote interest in British and Commonwealth wool. Interestingly, the social revolution brought about by the war had helped to launch wool into high fashion. It had previously been the province of the middle classes, with silk restricted to the upper classes and cotton the standard garb of labouring poor. The British Cotton Board also sought to rectify the situation by campaigning for a wider acceptance of its product. In the late fifties researchers came up with a blend that could be processed to make it uncrushable, and this did more than anything to make cotton fashionable for young-style summer dresses.

Linen weaving, another old-established British craft, was reinstated as a successful export product by the Irish designer Sybil Connolly, who also introduced Irish lawn, embroidered linen and crochet into the high-fashion catalogue. Her first collection was presented in 1950 in Dublin, where it was seen by representatives from the Philadelphia Fashion Group of America. Two years later she was invited to show her collection in Philadelphia and its instant success led to an increase in the supply of natural Irish weaves, especially banween – a chalk-white woollen material previously associated with tough country wear. By 1956 Miss Connolly had become one of the Irish Republic's prime exporters surpassing her countrymen John Cavanagh and Digby Morton in home popularity, since they, though supporting Irish tweeds, worked in London.

New fabrics and the development of good stores selling mass-produced goods inevitably effected changes in the whole fashion industry and not only in women's wear. Since before the war men's clothing in Britain had ranged from the elegance of Savile Row tailoring and the special occasion clothes of hire firms such as Moss Bros to their cheap copyists, the "Fifty-Shilling Tailors", who advertised their wares in bold black and white signboards displaying the letters FST. They disappeared almost overnight when the chain-stores John Collier and Burton's appeared on the scene, with their mass-produced suits that no company director need be ashamed to wear. For informal occasions grey flannel bags and navy blue serge gave way to sports jackets and slacks made from artificial fibres in more interesting weaves and hues than had been available to men before the war.

The next innovation occured when Cecil Gee, the first "trendy" menswear shop, opened its doors. Men at last had an image to cling to. Cecil Gee himself came from the tradition of Jewish tailoring in the East End of London, which was as exclusive in its way as Savile Row, though based on a different premise – the desire to reveal lavish expenditure rather than to conceal it. In 1946 he introduced the "American Look", which offered a slightly disreputable gangster image – double-breasted, wide-shouldered jackets, pin-striped and with large lapels and big drapes, shirts with long pointed collars, ties painted with pictures of cowboys and Indians or aeroplanes. This striking new look attracted long queues in the street outside his shop and he had to let his customers in six at a time. The immense popularity of the Cecil Gee style was based on the opportunity for flamboyant display it gave to men who had suffered for so long from the drabness of khaki. Yet it attracted strangely little publicity in the trade and national press, who did not recognize Cecil Gee as the first "pop" designer.

Gee's second "look" was the Italian mode he borrowed from Brioni, Italy's top designer, in the mid-fifties. The suit produced an effect of squatness and constriction. The jacket often rode up at the back (earning it the nickname "bum freezer") and the trousers were slightly too short, the buttons slightly too tight. The finishing touch was the characteristic pointed-toed shoe. This was not an elegant style but the "Italian" suit was a popular success, remaining in fashion for eight years and even spreading as far as Black Africa.

The British male was now beginning to take an interest in fashion again. The Men's Fashion Council reflected the changing tide in its 1953 fashion show, which thereafter became an annual event. Male modelling now acquired the status of a highly paid profession that only the most clean-limbed or rugged Anglo-Saxon could hope to enter. The look was typified by Michael Bentley and Roger Moore, who reached the top of their profession and set a style of modelling for many years to come. Bentley, though in fact American by birth, conformed to the ideal and his fan mail averaged 380 letters a week in his heyday. His appeal was based solely on his looks since he had none of the publicity build-up lavished on female models, who lived in the glare of the public eye and were envied and admired by every young magazine reader.

Barbara Goalen was the first influential model, initiating the cult of the glamour girl, the perfectly proportioned beauty who generated radiance and always seemed to be surrounded by the trappings of the affluent society that Britain was fast becoming. Models seemed to have everything that the press and media presented to the acquisitive as desirable – diamonds, a limousine, a yacht and suave escorts. The faces who set the fashion were those of Paulene Stone, Bronwen Pugh, Fiona Thyssen, Jean Dawnay, Shelagh Wilson, Marla Landi, and finally Suzy Parker, who sprang into the limelight at the very end of the fifties. A comparison between the photographs of these girls and the run-of-the-mill mannequins portrayed elsewhere in this book shows how badly the profession as a whole needed genuine modelling talent at this time.

The fifties girl cultivated a sophisticated look that placed her in the age range twenty-five to thirty-five, which was considered by fashion designers to be the ideal age. Very few designers were catering for teenagers, though the word had recently spread to Britain from the United States and many shops were beginning to open "young style" departments. On the whole, however, the teenage girl tended to dress like her mother, borrowing her bright red lipstick, stiletto heels and pencil-slim skirt for that important first evening out. For a completely new approach to fashions for the young she had to wait for Mary Quant.

Mary Quant's rise to international fame started in 1955, when she opened a shop in Chelsea, London, called Bazaar, which displayed eye-catching, even shocking designs aimed specifically at the adventurous young. The venture was an immediate success, for Quant clothes seemed doubly striking by contrast with the ubiquitous sack dress, which had strayed far from its *haute couture* origins to become the dowdy centre of the Englishwoman's wardrobe. Mary Quant's styles were both individual and colourful. She captured the spirit of a new forward-looking Britain and, in particular, the energy, independence and sexual liberation of its young women. Her efforts were paralleled in menswear by John Michael – another Chelsea-based designer – who brought a new excitement to men's shirts, ties and jackets.

54

A typically British sports outfit displayed at the "Britain Can Make It" exhibition at the Victoria and Albert Museum in 1946. It is a Dorville suit consisting of a beaver corduroy jacket and herringbone tweed skirt, and it is typical of the "country" look of the time./ *Radio Times Hulton Picture Library*

Left:
Norman Hartnell designed the Queen's wedding dress when in 1947, as Princess Elizabeth she married the Duke of Edinburgh, then Lieutenant Mountbatten. The bridal train stretched fourteen yards behind the princess and was embroidered with pearls and crystal in a milky way of small star-shaped blossoms. The motif was repeated on the dresses worn by the bridesmaids, who were each allowed twenty-three coupons for their outfits. The pages were allowed ten./
Keystone Press Agency

Above:
The year 1948 saw several versions of the back bustle theme in an attempt to vary the New Look. This dress was styled by Frederick Starke in a wool and nylon mixture called Frelon./*Keystone Press Agency*

Right:
Utility severity is still to be seen in these two suits for 1949. The girl wears a long-sleeved pinafore dress with a bib front. The man's suit is single-breasted, as this involved less cloth than a double-breasted suit./*The John French Photo Library*

Page Six

"Fay"   "Trudi"

Summer Frocks
from the Debutante Department

"FAY"/500
A typical example of one of our Utility Dresses, made in a delightfully patterned print, which cannot be repeated. Slight fullness in yoke on bodice, group of pleats front of skirt. Predominating colours : Dusky pink, turquoise, leaf green, lime, blue. Hip sizes 38, 40, 42 in.   52/11
Also the same print in a slightly different style, 55/4   (7 coupons)

"TRUDI"/500
A simple tailored Frock in check, shirt-maker style bodice, pleats in skirt. Colours : Pink, green and fawn, with a very feint black line running through, hip sizes 38 and 40 in. ; and a few in blue, hip size 40 in. only.   (7 coupons)   39/6

"GRENFELL"/500
One of three delightful styles made in spot crêpon. If desired belt can tie at back only, leaving panel front all in one, from which skirt with godet front flares prettily. For the other styles one has an all-round pleated skirt and high neckline, while the third is made with ten-gored skirt, bodice fastening through front and tiny white turn-back revers. Colours : Navy, china blue, corn, dusky pink, lime green, all with white spots. Hip sizes 36, 38, 40, 42 in.   (7 coupons)   4 gns.

"LISMORE"/500
An ideal Frock for any occasion. Pleated skirt and tucked bodice show to advantage the heavy crêpe in which it is made. Colours : Pastel blue, dusky pink, pastel green, Sèvres blue. Hip sizes 36, 38, 40 and 42 in.   (7 coupons)   £5 . 19 . 6

"Grenfell"   "Lismore"

Above:
Summer frocks from the debutante department at Marshall and Snelgrove in 1950. The frock on the left, with the identifying name "Grenfell", was made in soft crêpon and has a skirt with godet front flares. "Lismore", on the right, has a pleated skirt and tucked bodice in pastel shades of heavy crepe./*Marshall and Snelgrove*

Left:
A Norman Hartnell tailored dress featuring fine pleating at the hem-line and made of grey and white worsted (1951). The black wool coat is lined with check worsted to match the dress./*International Wool Secretariat*

Right:
A typical fifties image is seen in this Dereta gabardine spring suit with its pencil-slim skirt and overlapping collar. The sketch is by the leading fashion artist Francis Marshall, who drew for *Vogue* and followed the traditional style of fashion drawing. Hartnell described the process in his book *Silver and Gold:* "I sketch firstly the head, then roughly the limits of the figure, turning the body towards its right so that the left hip is foremost to my view. The hip is the focal point of nearly all draperies, clumps of flowers, panels, bucklings, sashes and bows. Then the arms, one akimbo and one outstretched to allow for the arrangement of the sleeves."/*Dereta*

Far left:
Glamour girl Fiona Campbell-Walker models a Digby Morton evening dress for 1951. The narrowing at the hem is relieved by fan-pleated net at the vent, matched at the hip. Digby Morton was an Irish designer whose early successes were in stylish tweed suits./
The John French Photo Library

Middle:
A pencil-slim suit by Julian Rose. A silk scarf clasped by a jewelled brooch is worn to relieve the stark outline./*The John French Photo Library*

Left:
Lachasse, who made this spun silk suit in 1952, was the head of a modest establishment in Mayfair that specialized in tailoring. Both Digby Morton and Hardy Amies trained there. The suit in the picture is embellished with a long stole emerging from under the revers to follow across the shoulders and finish at the back. It is lined with black taffeta./
The Silk and Rayon Users' Association

61

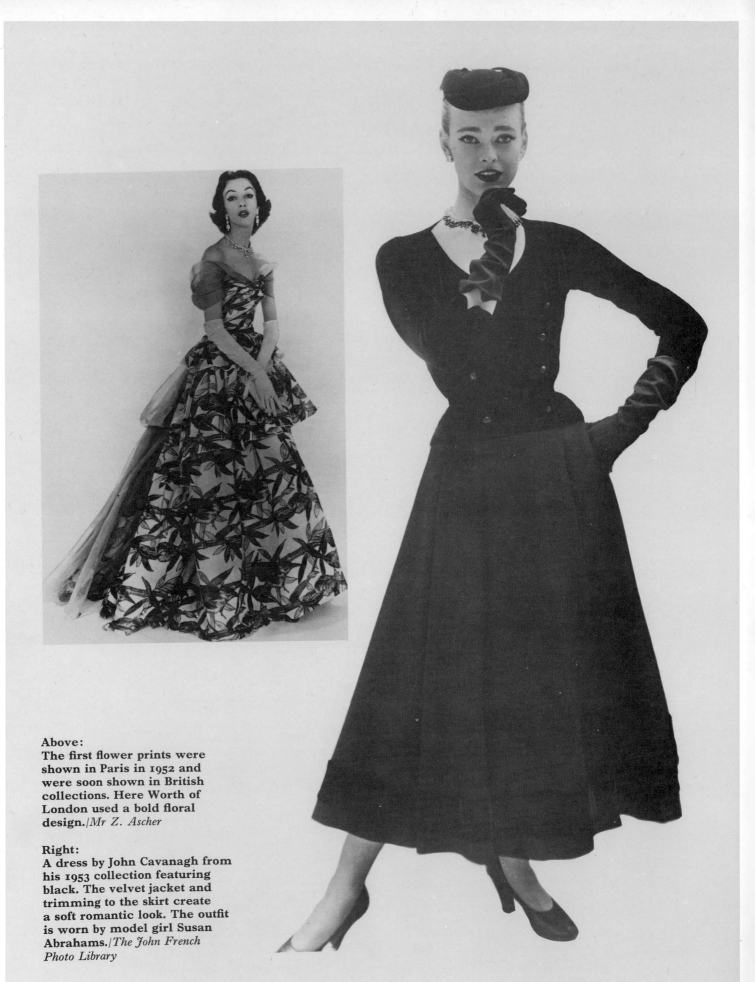

Above:
The first flower prints were shown in Paris in 1952 and were soon shown in British collections. Here Worth of London used a bold floral design./*Mr Z. Ascher*

Right:
A dress by John Cavanagh from his 1953 collection featuring black. The velvet jacket and trimming to the skirt create a soft romantic look. The outfit is worn by model girl Susan Abrahams./*The John French Photo Library*

A tailor-made by Charles Creed (1953). The house of Creed had specialized in riding habits in Queen Victoria's time and had moved to Paris to supply costumes to the Empress Eugénie and her retinue. Charles Creed had trained at the Rue de la Paix, bringing his knowledge back to grace English couture after the Second World War./
International Wool Secretariat

Left:
A Peter Russell suit of 1954, the year in which his house closed, showing the influence of the air-hostess image. The envelope bag matching the line of the skirt was very popular. Russell was of Irish origin and had grown up in India./
International Wool Secretariat

Far left:
The mass-production firm Polly Peck was one of the companies which specialized in converting Paris fashions for the home market. The picture shows a 1955 adaptation of a dress by Givenchy for the ready-to-wear trade./*Radio Times Hulton Picture Library*

Black and white contrasts were always popular for evening wear. Here a gathered organdie skirt in a stylized paisley design is topped by an off-the-shoulder bodice (1955)./
The John French Photo Library

Left:
This house gown for elegant evenings in daffodil-yellow wool is cut on fitted princess lines with very full skirt and flowing train. The short, wide sleeves are edged with a deep band of fur. From Hardy Amies's collection, 1956./ *International Wool Secretariat*

A cocktail dress of slipper satin printed in charred colours with a full flared skirt, by Victor Stiebel at Jacqmar (1956). Stiebel came from South Africa and had intended to study architecture at Cambridge. He came to costume design, like Hartnell, through designing for theatrical productions./*Jacqmar Ltd*

**Model Jean Dawnay dressed in
a Hollywood-inspired costume
of figure-revealing black dress
and white fur stole (1956.)/**
The John French Photo Library

Right:
Fashion editors were almost always attractive women with excellent taste in their own clothes. Here Jennifer Hocking, fashion editor of *Queen* magazine, models a Horrockses evening dress in 1956. The rage for large flower designs of this kind became vulgarized as the decade advanced. Big horizontal flowered prints were described as "bayadere".|
The John French Photo Library

Left:
An emerald-green velvet gown by Hartnell (1956). Hartnell said of the designing process; "Who can say exactly what gives rise to the creative impulse. A lingering melody or the cloying scent of lilies may suggest a romantic mauve dress for a sentimental matron. A wax-white magnolia in the moonlight is a debutante dancing at Hurlingham, a farmyard is redolent of sporting tweeds."|*Hartnell*

69

Left:
A typical party pair dressed for October 1957. (*Left*) Sweet-corn faille laced from heart to hemline; (*right*) olivine tulle dress with bodice wrapped in velvet ribbons./*The John French Photo Library*

Right:
The fashion for short coats worn over calf-length skirts was initiated by Paris. Camel hair coats such as this one, photographed in 1957, were very popular throughout the fifties. The large patent leather holdall is also typical/*The John French Photo Library*

Middle right:
A tiered evening gown by John Paterson (1958) offering a nostalgic echo of Victorian fashions. It is made in the finest denier of chiffon, so fine that only Paterson knew how to use it. The dress shows the degree of technical perfection possible in top London fashion houses./*Mr Z. Ascher*

Far right:
A spring tweed ready-made, easy-fitting and gently bloused at the back, with, as the advertisement says, "undating detail". Nevertheless it shows clear traces of the influences of the sack style. By Dereta (1958), sketched by Francis Marshall./*Dereta*

Left:
A London Town dress made in a new linen and terylene mixture called "Moygashel" (1958)./*Moygashel and Springback*

Far left:
Paulene Stone, another of Britain's top models, wearing a plain suit marketed by the chain store Richard Shops (1959)./*The John French Photo Library*

Above:
Three of Mary Quant's early designs. From left to right, a pinafore sack-style dress in grey flannel with round neck and box pleats (1958), a round-neck A line pinafore dress with a kick pleat at the centre front (1960) and a V-neck button-up shirt-dress with cutaway armholes and two pockets just above the hem

(1960). All three outfits were designed to be worn with blouses or polo-neck jumpers. The drawings have immediate impact and it is easy to see why young buyers found Quant clothes so appealing./*Mary Quant Ltd*

Above left:
Barbara Goalen, queen of the models, portrayed with the popular male model Roger Moore in 1951./*The John French Photo Library*

Above:
The timeless look of the British upper-class male. Functions at which gentlemen were expected to wear evening dress for dinner were still frequent during the forties and fifties, and a man who in the seventies would have occasion to bring out his dinner jacket only once every one to two months was probably wearing it once a week in those days. White-tie occasions have since become extremely rare./*Moss Bros*

Bottom far left:
A maroon velvet smoking jacket worn with a school or college tie. Such ties were worn as a sort of poster advertising group membership./*Moss Bros*

Bottom left:
The typical city gentleman; well-tailored coat with velvet collar, bowler hat, gloves and the obligatory umbrella. The picture was taken in 1955 but it epitomizes the about-town appearance throughout the forties and fifties./*Moss Bros*

Left:
Country casual wear for the gentleman. Sports jackets were just coming into fashion in the fifties and were adapted for ordinary use from the sports field./*Moss Bros*

A 1952 cartoon shows how far men's fashions had developed from the beaux of more flamboyant days. The duffel coat entered men's wardrobes after the war and was seen everywhere in the fifties. These coats had first been made at Duffel in Flanders in the eighteenth century and were later sent out to the colonies because their thick tufted nap made them hard wearing. This quality made the fabric ideal for wartime coats and after the war large supplies of government-surplus garments were sold off to the general public./*Marshall and Snelgrove*

Thank goodness that after centuries . . .

of absurdity in men's dress .

sanity and taste are at last combined . . .

in 1952.

Specially drawn for " THE SKETCH " by ffolkes.

Plaids and tartans were seen
everywhere in the United
States. They originated in the
brightly coloured shirts of the
lumberjacks, who wore them
so that they could be spotted
easily while they worked in the
forests. Here an all-American
girl wears a yellow, red, black
and white plaid skirt with
matching cutaway jacket (1947).
Keystone Press Agency

American Casual

The Second World War marks a watershed in the history of American fashion. Up to 1940 it was the dream of every young married woman to be taken to Paris on her honeymoon to order a set of clothes for her trousseau, for there and only there was the unquestioned centre of chic. American clothes were entirely based on news from Paris, this reliance dating back to the days of the War of Independence when cotton and tobacco planters transferred their allegiance from the old mother country and ordered their clothes direct from France in exchange for shipments of crops. But the events of 1940 threw the United States back on her own resources, since the British fashion trade was as yet too immature to assume worldwide supremacy. The result was the gradual evolution of a distinctive American look that grew out of the designers' study of their own heritage and psychology. By the end of the fifties American fashions had achieved transatlantic recognition and clothing had become the third largest industry in the United States.

The American look developed out of several different strands of thinking, each running parallel with the other alongside the vast technological revolution caused by the innovations of the war years. From the first it was a practical rather than a romantic look, culling its ideas from such sources as the pretty print dresses and patchworks worn by pioneer women of the 1860s, frilled cottons from neighbouring Mexico, plaid shirts borrowed from Canadian lumberjacks, the fringed leather of the American Indian, the stitched and riveted functionalism of the modern workman's overalls, the dress of the mid west cowboys and even the nationwide preoccupation with the fabulous adventures of comic-strip heroes. Characters such as Superman, Flash Gordon and the Phantom, with their angular features and gleaming appearance, gave rise to a brave-new-worldish garb that owed nothing to European influences, with its coloured tights and matching hooded cloaks, garish shirts and tight buckled belts.

The early successes began in a modest way, in a small basement shop in Washington Square. Here an American businessman, Mr Phelps, and his wife, sold hand-made belts and bags, the belts broad and buckled with brass and the bags slung on a shoulder strap. To give some individuality to these otherwise undistinguished accessories, the Phelpses used badges depicting brass eagles and crossed rifles dating back to the Civil War, which they displayed prominently as part of the clasp mechanism. The idea caught on so rapidly that they ran out of original Civil War badges and had to manufacture copies, for here at last was something with a nationalistic slant exactly suited to the mood of the patriotic girl in 1943. At the same time, clothing reflected the wartime mood, so that in the United States, as in Britain, civilian costume was in tune with official wear. The difference was that in the United States this did not degenerate into drab uniform, for there was still enough fabric for gathered "ballerina"-length skirts bound at the waist by a velvet corselet belt and worn with pretty cotton blouses. This was the customary wear of the young dancing maiden, who compromised with a halfway hem to match the halfway formality of all wartime social occasions.

After the war, European visitors to New York were astonished by the general sense of well-being they saw everywhere. Cecil Beaton, writing about his trip in 1945, told *Vogue* readers, "I thought I had never seen such wonderful young women with their towering Marie Antoinette hairdos, topped with artificial flowers, plump with healthy porcelain complexions, with high pointed bosoms and 'cuisses'. In fashionable restaurants the women were wearing, on their heads, enormous platters strewn with ostrich plumes or roses. It was as if the war had never been!" But New York was the centre of the clothing industry and what held good there was not necessarily true of the rest of the United States. Many fashions that started their life in the cultural capital took three or four years to reach the west coast and never travelled to some parts of the mid west at all. It should, therefore, be remembered that any dates given in this book relate to the time of origin of a fashion, which does not necessarily coincide with the peak of its general popularity. Made-to-measure houses outside New York were rare, the only exception being California, which had Howard Greer in San Francisco and Adrian in Hollywood as well as Mr John, who made hats for all the most famous stars of the screen. All three designers eventually came to New York, where a new atmosphere had been created by the return to the United States of the Chicago-born couturier Main R. Bocher. He had been running a fashion house in Paris for many years, under the name Mainbocher, and he now brought back with him the confidence and professional know-how needed to boost native talent. Few could afford to be dressed by him personally, for as the *New York Times* said: "Mainbocher not only makes a woman look as if she had money, but as if she had had it all her life and her father before her."

Mainbocher's clothes were indeed expensive and in any case his female compatriots were on the whole too busy to be over-fastidious about their dress, as he himself noted: "American women are always in a hurry. They want to pick a dress today and wear it yesterday. Fittings make them fidgety." Dior noted the same tendency on his trip to the United States in 1947, believing that it was the main difference between American and French women. He was surprised that the former preferred to buy a multitude of mediocre things to a few carefully chosen ones: "She prefers three new dresses to one beautiful one. She never hangs back from making a choice, knowing perfectly well that her fancy will be of short duration and the dress which she is in the process of buying will be jettisoned very soon." It was partly this fact about feminine psychology that precipitated the improvements in mass-producing techniques.

A number of well-established and original designers were already working for the ready-to-wear market in the United States, which even before the war had attracted the talents of original designers such as Tom Brigance, Claire McCardle, Claire Potter and Norman Norell. They were now joined by Hattie Carnegie, Charles James and Bonnie Cashin. Bonnie Cashin's fame began in 1950 with her "layered look", the idea being to create clothes that went together, like a set of Chinese boxes, so that garments could be piled on or peeled off according to climatic changes, the figure always looking neat and trim. This attitude to the need for versatility was later to give rise to the "mix 'n match" separates that flooded the world's market in the sixties. Bonnie Cashin's scope was broad, ranging from individually fitted outfits of Chanel-like classicism, to garments designed to meet the demands of mass-production. The second group included designs for frontier dresses, wild west ponchos, pocahontas dresses, Japanese-style "Noh" coats and a variety of sports separates.

The great advantage of separates from the manufacturer's point of view is that they are extremely adaptable and can therefore cope with problems of sizing. Like any other woman, the average American female did not conform to the bust/waist/hips ideal of the 10, 12, 14, 16 sizing groups. Sizing in the United States was far in advance of Europe, as the much larger geographical area involved made it economical for manufacturers to provide thirty-three different sizing groups, while London stores were doing well if they carried as many as ten different sizes on their racks. (In fact some of the American variations involved only a different hem length, as three alternative lengths were commonly offered for one bust/hip measurement). American leadership in the matter of sizing was recognized by the rest of the industry, who adopted the method of numbering. A group of French businessmen acknowledged their American counterparts' supremacy by crossing the Atlantic in 1947 to study methods of marketing. They also examined the question of dress construction, since American manufacturers had effectively solved the problem of translating a garment in the round into something capable of being cut on the flat with vast scissors cutting out dozens of pieces at a time.

Buyers still went to Paris, keeping an eagle eye open for details that could be incorporated into a machine-made garment and avoiding models that relied heavily on expensive fabric for their effect. The arrival of the resultant copies in the shops each season was timed to coincide with publicity in the "glossies" (notably *Vogue* and *Harper's Bazaar*), which had an enormous influence on fashion in the United States, as well as in Britain and France. Both magazines, while encouraging home industries (American *Vogue* had a trade pullout that gave advice to manufacturers on where and how to sell their goods), nevertheless promoted the best ideas coming out of Europe, giving full credit to the renaissance of Paris under Dior. American *Vogue's* editor, Edna Woolman Chase, initiated the system of giving the originating fashion house a credit on the new garment and Carmel Snow, editor of *Harper's Bazaar*, was made a Chevalier of the Légion d'Honneur in France in 1949 as a compliment to her influence in promoting French fashion.

Alongside the éclat of France's New Look, whose unpopularity in the western states has already been noted, America was developing her own shirtwaister, which was to become the hallmark of fashion for many years. The first shirtwaisters were worn with Mexican-inspired black espadrilles, their ribbons crisscrossing round the ankles. The appeal of the shirtwaister lay in its practicality and its suitability for all age groups; one manufacturer even produced matching dresses for mother and her small daughter.

Children were indeed enjoying a far-reaching sartorial revolution in this period. The new attitude to children's clothes originated in the States, where children have always been regarded as of more consequence than in Europe. They are encouraged early in life to participate in the conversations and activities of their elders and are brought up to assert their sense of individuality, an attitude that was soon reflected in their dress. Children's clothes were at last being designed to stand up to the rigours of childhood, rather than as miniature replicas of their parents' dress. The revolution began in babyhood, with the stretch cover-all suit made of a cotton and nylon mix that "grew" with the baby. Instead of being swaddled in constraining wraps the baby was now allowed to thrash and kick about at will. The idea was the brainchild of Walter Artzt in the late fifties (he did not bring the garment to Britain until 1959). As the baby grew into a toddler, he or she wore sweater, pull-on garments, workman-style dungarees and all kinds of knockabout playsuits and slacks.

The next step was perhaps the inevitable backlash: for the first time in fashion history clothes that had originally been intended for children climbed up the age ladder into the adult wardrobe. The fifties saw American college girls wearing childlike circular skirts – often appliquéd with such nursery motifs as a pink felt poodle – plain or tartan culottes worn with a blouse and side-tied neckerchief and white bobby socks worn with plimsolls. The hair would be tied up in a youthful pony tail or allowed to hang loose, for American girls had thrown away their hats after the war and they have never again been in general use. In 1952 Vogue gave official recognition to this teenage fashion market by starting a "Young Idea" feature aimed at the seventeen to twenty-five age group. Statistics had shown that two-thirds of the female population in the United States were under thirty – the age group with few commitments and money to spend on clothes.

Young style clothing consisted of three main strands. In the first place there were the ingénue, all-American kids, the bobby-soxers, who dressed like little girls; the crinolines and hooped skirts of the late fifties appealed to this group, who delighted in displaying tiny waists and a flurry of frilled petticoats. Then came the "tomboys" who wore blue jeans and all manner of variations on the wild west theme to express their nostalgia for a vanished America redolent of danger and daring. Some 6,000 picture houses relayed Westerns every week, Shane (1953) being one of the most popular, the box-office proceeds topping $8,000,000 (about £2,860,000). The third group consisted of teenagers who worshipped the sophistication of the Hollywood filmstar. Girls graduating from eighth grade into high school would wear their first high-heeled shoes and a tight, pencil-slim skirt with a banlon sweater – with two or three buttons left undone to emulate the Hollywood "cleavage". (The word had

first made its appearance in the fashion vocabulary in the mid-fifties, when stars such as Jayne Mansfield and Marilyn Monroe adopted décolleté garments.) Bright red lipstick added the finishing touch and the hair was backcombed into a bouffant "chrysanthemum" shape.

Jane Russell was the first of the "sweater girls", appearing in 1946 in The Outlaw wearing a bra designed by none other than the future millionaire recluse Howard Hughes to create a pointed uplift to the bosom. The film was banned for several years by the Hays Office (Board of Censors), who were shocked by its overt sexual display. But the most famous of the fifties sweater girls was, of course, Marilyn Monroe, who inevitably wore pullovers that accentuated the shape of her bust. The details of Marilyn's dimensions were published the world over. Punch, from across the Atlantic, noted, with its characteristic wry humour, "Today in the battle for fame and fortune, it is the bust which is in the van. Hips bring up, with encircling movements, reinforcements from the rear; legs, although not actually non-combatant, are held in reserve; semi-secret weapons." On the strength of her figure Marilyn rocketed from obscurity to become the pin-up girl of the decade. Her shape was soon the ideal of young people (and older people) in all film-viewing countries, leading to the cult of the vital statistics. A boom in the foundations industry was inevitable: waist-cynchers, padded bras and hip belts were an important feature of feminine wardrobe, and even in France bras were labelled with the slogan "le véritable busty-look americain".

The sweaters of le busty-look ranged from the ordinary to the fanciful. Jumpers would be embroidered with paillettes or stamped all over with rhinestones, sequins, beads and chiffon ribbons, for one result of the Hollywood influence was to create a popular market for gaudy display. Cheap plastic poppet necklaces in bright colours – "pathy pink" and "taffy blue" imitated the filmstar's pearls and fake furs were stand-ins for Hollywood mink. It was in the fifties that the fur of mink acquired its kudos. Since it took seventy to a hundred skins to make one mink coat, this status symbol element was far from surprising in pre-ecology days – after all, its high cost was a measure of its wearer's success. Mink definitely stood for glamour, for spotlights and gala openings.

Fake furs, on the other hand, were made of nylon – one of the many uses in the clothing industry of this versatile product. Nylon had been discovered in 1929 by W. H. Carothers, who stumbled on it by accident when he was trying to make synthetic rubber from coal, air, water and vegetable oils. But it was not used for clothing for another ten years, when the first "nylons" replaced the shiny silk stockings that had made women's legs ugly since the twenties. By the end of the forties, synthetic yarn production in the

States exceeded that of the rest of the world with Japan following closely in second place. The chief advantages were its cheapness, and the fact that it insulated its wearer against both heat and cold, was washable, light in weight and non-crushable. Fashion miracles were achieved when artificial fibres were skilfully blended with natural ones to exploit the good qualities of each. Stretchable cloth gave birth to ideas in form-hugging garments for men, women and children, all of whom enjoyed the luxurious feeling of a perfect fit. New products such as Orlon, Banlon, Acrilan, Dacron and Poplin revolutionized all aspects of fashion, particularly in the lingerie sphere. They also completely changed people's habits and standards of cleanliness. By the end of the forties even the busiest office girl could wear clean nylon underclothes and nightwear every day, since the previous day's clothes could be washed, dried and ready for rewear in a matter of hours.

Artificial fibres also had an important influence on men's outer wear, for the first nylon shirts appeared immediately after the war. They were very expensive in those days, but drip-dry Poplin quickly overtook cotton in popularity. This led in turn to the emergence of a fashion for coloured shirts, since they were easy to manufacture and simple to launder.

Two images had emerged for men – the hard and the soft. Tough dress emulated the gorilla silhouette of the comics' criminal, with heavy jacket, limp slouch hat, slim drainpipe trousers and small shoes. This was the look that Marlon Brando popularized in *On the Waterfront* and it was copied in thousands of docker-style jackets worn by the youth of America with their tough denim miner's levis. New heroes were sought and quirks of fashion followed each other in rapid succession. One of the most dramatic was the Davy Crockett outfit (often reduced simply to the trapper hat), for Walt Disney had brought Davy back into the limelight in 1955. Much of the drama was due to the furore raised by the anti-vivisection lobby, who demanded to know the source of the fur tails hanging down from the back of the hats. Nevertheless it was very popular among schoolchildren both in North America and Europe, and even in some parts of Asia.

The soft look was represented by the dress of the European city businessman, which persisted in spite of its unsuitability for the American climate. Advertisements invited aspiring tycoons to purchase "relaxed formals with masculine magnetism", assuring them that their evening would be "far more enchanted when you go elegantly formal" with pull-on shoes giving "that lean, restrained, Patrician look". The American contribution to the uninspiring lounge suit was to liven it up with shocking pink or Hawaiian flowered shirts, ready-made cummerbunds with matching clip-on ties and braces alluringly decorated with acrobats or dancing girls. In 1950 the Costume Institute of the Metropolitan Museum in New York staged an exhibition entitled "Adam in the Looking Glass", which aimed to make men more aware of the image they presented. Twelve well-known women designers were invited to work their will on men's suits, hats and shirts, but few of them dared to depart from the grey-black bleakness demanded by male conservatism. There were a few experiments at initiating more convenient clothing, as for example in the bank of Tomkins County Trust Company, Ithaca, New York, where the clerks were uniformed in white Bermudas or plaid shorts and white open neck shirts during the hot summer of 1955. As everyone was dressed in the same way the experiment was to some extent successful, if a little self-conscious, for it is hard to visualize an ageing pot-bellied businessman quite at his ease in youthful knee-high socks.

Somewhere in between the two images was the casual sporting look that originated on the university campus when the young men back from the Korean War threw convention to the winds and the new mood of "anything goes" was reflected in non-serious clothing. They took to wearing sports jackets of fancy tweed threaded with green Lurex, grey flannels, reversible waistcoats (vests) – Paisley one side and a bright plain colour the other – and button-down shirts. Ties were whittled down to a thickness of one and a half inches, their slimness possibly marking a protest against high school dress codes, which enforced the wearing of ties. There was also the Ivy League look, which popularized soft woven jackets and pull-on Norwegian shoes. Bermuda shorts were soon being worn on campus, the first perfectly tailored ones making news in 1953. During the rage for Bermudas and their successors, Jamaicas, quite a few brave young men even attended country club dances attired in shorts and dinner jackets.

But for the most part American male costume echoed European drabness. Indigenous influences did occasionally make themselves felt but they did not successfully encroach on the businessman's wardrobe. On the other hand, women's, and particularly girl's, dress, was influencing both the western and the eastern world. The youth of all American-aided countries were greedily devouring American films and comics and catching glimpses of the habits and costumes of a society they sought to emulate. America began the forties with only a few fashion ideas of her own; by the end of the fifties she led the rest of the world.

Above:
American fashions for summer 1942. Coloured cotton frocks were popular and many were cut on the shirtwaist lines like the one on the left, which appeared in British stores at a cost of £1.32 (about $5.28). Americans, like the British, favoured skirts with dungaree bibs. The shoes seen on the figure on the right are made of strips to save on leather, and are mounted on a wedge heel./ *Radio Times Hulton Picture Library*

Four American GIs watch a model in the salon of Jean Patou in Paris in 1944, a year when Parisian designers were trying to recapture the American market./*Keystone Press Agency*

Left:
Hollywood actress Lilli Palmer
wears an evening gown by the
Californian designer Adrian,
who dressed many of America's
filmstars. The gown is made of
sheer black chiffon softly
gathered over a starched lace
bodice and ending in a stiff
peplum over the hips. The long
black crêpe skirt is slit at the
back to give freedom for
dancing./*Keystone Press Agency*

The five separate trends of the
American look in 1946, all
giving an effect of youth,
independence and simplicity;
a) shirtwaisted girls wearing a
Phelps bag inspired by the
equipment of Civil War
soldiers; b) the design of prim
gingham frocks, which gave an
old-worldly, little girl look,
harked back to the pioneer
women of the covered waggon
era; c) ballerina-length skirts
introduced by the Russian-born
designer Valentina, who
introduced into the wardrobe
the new enthusiasm for ballet
that was sweeping the United
States; d) farm labourers'
overalls gave the idea of
tough-looking cotton clothes;
e) comic-strip heroes were
responsible for wollen tights,
hoods and tightly belted coats./
Harper's Bazaar

84

Minnie Mouse, though created in the thirties, became a cult figure of the late fifties with the beginnings of "pop" culture. Transfers of Minnie and Mickey were stamped on T-shirts, bags, badges and scarves. These garments were intended to provoke amusement, reinforcing the sense of fun and fantasy that made Disneyland (founded in 1955) so popular./*Walt Disney Productions Ltd*

Superman, the comic hero who
influenced teenage fashions./
National Periodical Publications Inc

Three outfits inspired by influences from neighbouring Mexico. The wide cummerbund, off-the-shoulder blouse and espadrilles of the two girls (*left and centre*) show Spanish-American overtones. They are also in tune with the New Look skirt fullness that was hitting the headlines in 1947, when the two outfits were made. The hairstyles show echoes of American primitive paintings, which had a tremendous influence on fashion. The ever-popular polka-dotted dress (*right*) was made in 1949./*Keystone Press Agency*

Right:
Crêpe tunic dress with accordion pleated flares, a detail typical of 1949. Designed by Californian Irene Bury./ *Fox Photos*

Below:
Girl's pleated skirt for 1949 by Trude of California, made to match mother's skirt. The drawstring at the waist pulls the garment flat for easy pressing./*Fox Photos*

A postwar creation in black silk faille taffeta by the Anglo-American designer Charles James, who was one of the few couturiers who was himself capable of making every detail of the clothes he designed. Charles James had a far-reaching influence on the wholesale dress trade./ *Keystone Press Agency*

Roy Rogers, known as "King of the Cowboys", and his wife arrive at the airport in Wild West jacket with Red Indian markings./*Keystone Press Agency*

Left:
Capri style pants and tight cummerbund with ruffled shirt from Hollywood showing inspiration from Spanish costume, emphasized by the sombrero hat (1953)./*Keystone Press Agency*

Below:
The Levi-Strauss colophon characterizes the return to functional dress of American youth, who recreated this image a hundred years later. The original "levis" were made for the gold rush miners in 1850 and remained the practical garb of labourers. In the early fifties they made their appearance on college campuses across the continent. Only blue men's jeans were available in the fifties, though both sexes wore them, and it was not until 1960 that new colours came in and jeans were made with girl's figures in mind./*Levi-Strauss Ltd*

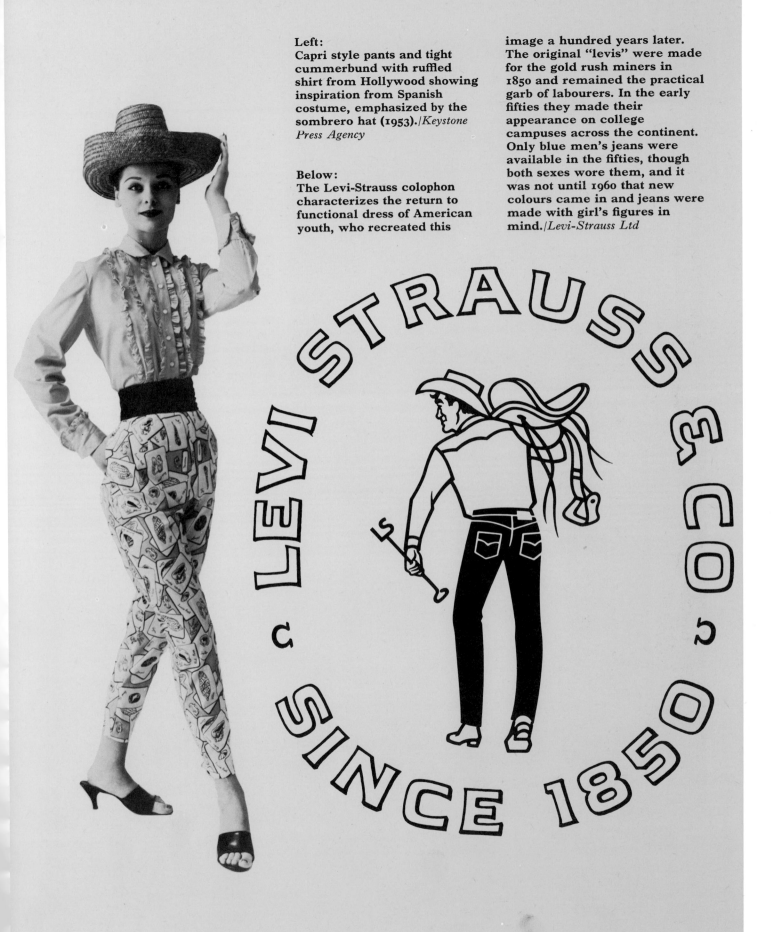

Above:
The Meeting by Pop Art painter Richard Lindner (1953) shows a stylization of clothing of the time./*William and Norma Copley Foundation*

In 1955 Walt Disney promoted the film *Davy Crockett*. The frontier hero became the new teenage idol, creating a rage for trapper-style dress. Moccasins, fringed jackets and trousers, and above all the fur hat with a tail at the back were seen in all parts of the world, and were especially popular with children./*Walt Disney Production Ltd*

Jayne Mansfield exhibits the "cleavage" (a new word for an old idea), for Hollywood filmstars had brought bust display back into fashion. She also carries a miniature dog, associated since the eigtheenth century with a life of leisure and therefore the perfect accessory for the wealthy./ *Keystone Press Agency*

96

Favourite pin-up girls of the forties were Lana Turner and Jane Russell, whose pictures were sent to the armed forces. The popular style for pin-up pictures was a swimsuit pose with romantic lighting./ *Twentieth-Century Fox, United Artists Inc*

E53-4. POR. 1

98

Fifties faces who set the fashion for looks included Diana Dors and the incomparable Marilyn Monroe, seen here in a publicity picture for *The Seven-Year Itch* **(1954)**./*ABC Films, Twentieth-Century Fox*

The face of the decade, Marilyn Monroe./
Twentieth Century Fox

The male heroes – adored by women and emulated by men – included Tab Hunter, James Dean and Gene Kelly. James Dean's romantic looks were reinforced by his tragic accidental death the year after *Rebel without a Cause* (1955), from which this shot was taken. Gene Kelly's sporting image, complete with jockey cap, was familiar college campus wear./
Paramount Pictures, Warner Brothers

Right:
American fabric design
followed European trends. This
dress material for 1945 shows
the standard preoccupation with
small drawings and penlike
flourishes./*Cotton Board*

Two girls model rock-and-roll slacks for summer 1957. They are three-quarter length and tapered, with a zip at the bottom to give extra tightness. The blouses are borrowed from men's shirts./*Keystone Press Agency*

Teenage Rock

The fifties saw the rise of a new generation, a group of young people who had been born after the war, or were too young to remember it, and who therefore did not share with their elders the memory of an experience that had affected a whole way of life. The new group was "in revolt" – as the younger generation has of course always been – but it was a larger and more assertive group than any previous youth movement, looking within itself for its leaders. The war had sadly reduced the capacity of the bridging age group, who had one foot in the old world and another in the new, so the whole burden of groping towards a new ethos fell on the young. They began by rejecting the old order of things wholesale, in true "angry young man" fashion. John Osborne was only twenty-six when his play *Look Back in Anger* (1955) was successfully produced personifying the new "protesting" hero of the age, whose impact was reinforced in the same year by James Dean in *Rebel Without a Cause*.

The activities of the teenage and post-teen group became headline news because young people were fast becoming economically independent and in the years between leaving school and marriage were able to enjoy a freedom and opulence that their parents had never known. The generation gap was now as wide as it had ever been. As a lecturer (Mr G. Prys William) at the London School of Economics expressed it: "If you were given a Hottentot to bring up I think you would have a bit of a job because I do not think you would begin to understand how the Hottentot mind works. As far as we are concerned, I think this teenage group is a Hottentot group." In the first place it was a spendthrift group, with an enormous daily expenditure. Its insatiable appetite for novelty and the desire to imitate the other members of the peer group made the teenage market one that advertisers and manufacturers could not afford to ignore. "With new teenagers arriving at the rate of half a million a year," wrote the *Draper's Record*, "the teenage trade cannot be treated as a sideline . . ." Department stores set up special teenage boutiques and new magazines appealed to an ever-lower age range since, in London and New York

at least, romance comics were commonly being read by girls of eleven; at thirteen they were using make-up and by fifteen they were confidently expecting to "go steady". Changes of outfit were seasonal and no self-respecting teenager would wear the same clothes two years running.

For boys, the desire to dress with style was a reaction against the shabbiness that had become patriotic in the days of rationing. A yearning for lost elegance began to express itself in a taste for Edwardian clothing among young men about town from about 1949 onwards. Many of the "New-Edwardians", as they were called, belonged to an aristocratic milieu with fast-vanishing privileges and they expressed their nostalgia for an era in which their class had had all the advantages in their choice of clothes. They went for "saucy-cut toggery" (as Savile Row called it) – narrow trousers with raised seams, step-collared or brocaded waistcoats, skirted jackets with a single or double vent at the back, coats with turned-back velvet cuffs and velvet collars. The most stylish New-Edwardian was the English dressmaker Bunny Rogers, who brought colour into male costume – golds and crimsons, pinks and purples and plenty of accessories, monocles, watch-chains and diamond tie-pins.

Yet although the Edwardian cult was restricted to a relatively small circle of people, it had far-reaching effects. Its most characteristic feature was a narrowing down of the line, and it was this that became vulgarized and popularized by the "neo-Neo-Edwardians", – the "teddy boys". The movement began in London's East End in 1952, formed by the semi-skilled youths of the working class who had time and money on their hands. They formed gangs and lurked at street corners or in "caffs" looking for opportunities to let off steam by violent behaviour. Often they were impatient with the restrictions of childhood, yet they were not ready for the responsibilities of adulthood. This led to uncontrolled frustration that expressed itself in vicious outbursts. They egged each other on to reckless adventures to demonstrate their bravery, often seeking the approval of a "teddy girl", who would transfer her allegiance from one member of a gang to another according to who showed the greatest daring. They had no concern for morals, politics or philosophy, but about style they were fanatical, using it as a way of illustrating contempt for authority.

Teddy boy dress soon became an obligatory uniform in certain urban areas, for no young man cared to walk home in clothes that indicated that he held himself aloof from the teddy boy team. In any case many non-violent youths chose teddy boy clothing because it represented a breakaway from convention. Traditionally it consisted of a drape – a knee-length, single-breasted jacket with padded shoulders, which gave a "tough guy" bulk to the figure – a stiff shirt and embroidered waistcoat, skin-tight drainpipe jeans, two-inch thick crêpe-soled shoes (known as "brothel creepers") worn with fluorescent pink, green or yellow socks, and a "slim jim" or bootlace tie. Brass rings were worn on the fingers, for decorative as well as destructive purposes, and a flick-knife was generally carried in the back jeans pocket. The hair was carefully greased, with sideburns plunging well past the earlobes, and the top was swept up in a quiff at the front and dragged back at the sides in a style known as the DA or "duck's arse". Not only was this dress intended to display toughness, it also possessed a definite mating appeal – very necessary in view of the postwar phenomenon of an increased ratio of boys to girls. Indeed part of its importance is that it put sexuality back into menswear for the first time since the early nineteenth century. The girls loved it and answered with short fitted jackets worn over a skin-tight black sweater and a calf-length clinging skirt, which were designed to exhibit plenty of bust and hip movement.

By 1956 the costume was changing, as an East Ender explained in a letter to the *Daily Mirror:* "Crêpe-soled creepers and drainpipe trousers are *out* for the really smart boy nowadays. We wear trousers with turnups eighteen inches round, and black leather shoes with highly polished toe-caps. Long hair is finished too. The favourite cut today is a short crop 'Marlon Brando' or a short style with a quiff falling over the forehead." The shoes were the sharply pointed winkle-pickers that reached Britain from Italy in 1957. Such outfits were not cheap and full teddy boy regalia could cost more than £100 ($280) with the result that sporting new outfits became a conspicuous way of displaying class membership. At Tottenham Royal, the largest teddy boy dance centre in North London, girl partners would put a price on everything a boy was wearing before consenting to dance with him. He would nonchalantly stand in front of her combing his hair and staring at her with hooded eyes, inviting her on to the floor with no more than a flick of his head. The wheel had turned full circle from the days of the eighteenth-century dandies and belles, whose aim had

been to exhibit their wealth on their person and thus demonstrate their superiority to the lower orders. Now it was the "lower orders" who were in the van as far as fashion was concerned, and they wore their outfits as a badge of arrival.

The teddy boy costume spread from Britain to the rest of the western-influenced world, – and even to the Soviet Union, where it must have formed a strange contrast to the ubiquitous overalls. By 1958, however, the movement had begun to fade as teenagers were gripped by the influences of pop culture. In the United States teddy boys were paralleled by the "greasers" and "rockers", who wore similar clothing except that the drape became a leather jacket, which was sometimes worn with leather trousers. The largest accessory in the greaser's equipage was a shining motorbike, on which he lavished a great deal of attention and which was later to become the symbol of the "tough guy" image. The greasers also congregated in gangs and were almost always to be seen chewing gum and bringing out a comb to perfect their coiffure.

"Dudes" were another kind of American dandy of the mid-fifties, who marked themselves off from the greasers by wearing clean white socks with highly polished white buckskin shoes. Shoes became the subject of fetishistic interest, favourites being the black or brown "penny loafers", so called because of the design across the top of the shoe, into which a penny could be inserted, the black and white saddle Oxfords or the tan-coloured threadneedles, which had a steel plate in the sole and made a tapping noise as the wearer walked. Jackets were fastened with five buttons and the trousers, which were pleated at the waistband, had turnups. The outfit was enlivened by gaudy or jazzy accessories such as polka dot hats, wampam belts (made of coloured beads) or Indian beaded bags. Popular songs of the time reflected the preoccupations of the clothes-conscious teenager and titles such as "White Sports Coat", "Blue Suede Shoes" or "Tan Shoes with Pink Shoelaces" were soon climbing up the charts.

Clothing was one thing to spend money on; popular music was another. The first appearance of the micro-groove plastic disc in the United States in 1950 caused a revolution in the quality as well as the quantity of sound reproduction. By 1954 record sales were four times the prewar level and were still growing fast. The type of music was beginning to change too. During the forties and early fifties there was no teenage music as such, but all age groups enjoyed the soft warm sound of the big bands, who offered sentimental songs about stardust, roses and bleeding hearts, presenting to the audience a strictly formal image attired in either stiff tail coats or spangled and sequined lounge suits. There were few heroes, the reputation of the band attracting larger numbers than the singers themselves, who were

A studio portrait of the actress
Esther Williams in 1947. She is
wearing a peasant style
gathered skirt which owes its
influence to the United States'
neighbour, Mexico. The padded
shoulders and side tucks on
the blouse were typical./
Kobal Collection

This brilliant poppy colour was Dior's trade mark and it was known as "Rouge Dior". The dress shows a fined down version of the New Look with the inevitable dropped shoulder and a billow of gathers about the waist (1949)./Harper's Bazaar

Off-the-peg clothes for 1947 all showing the severity of cut demanded by the times. The top row are "stand by" suits, middle, all day dresses, and bottom, coat./Harper's Bazaar

Details of fabric design typical of the two decades. In the forties small abstract patterns composed typically of dots and dashes were popular. In the fifties stylized flowers were among the most favoured designs. This example shows the use of colour on a colour background which was an innovation of 1956./Mr Z. Ascher

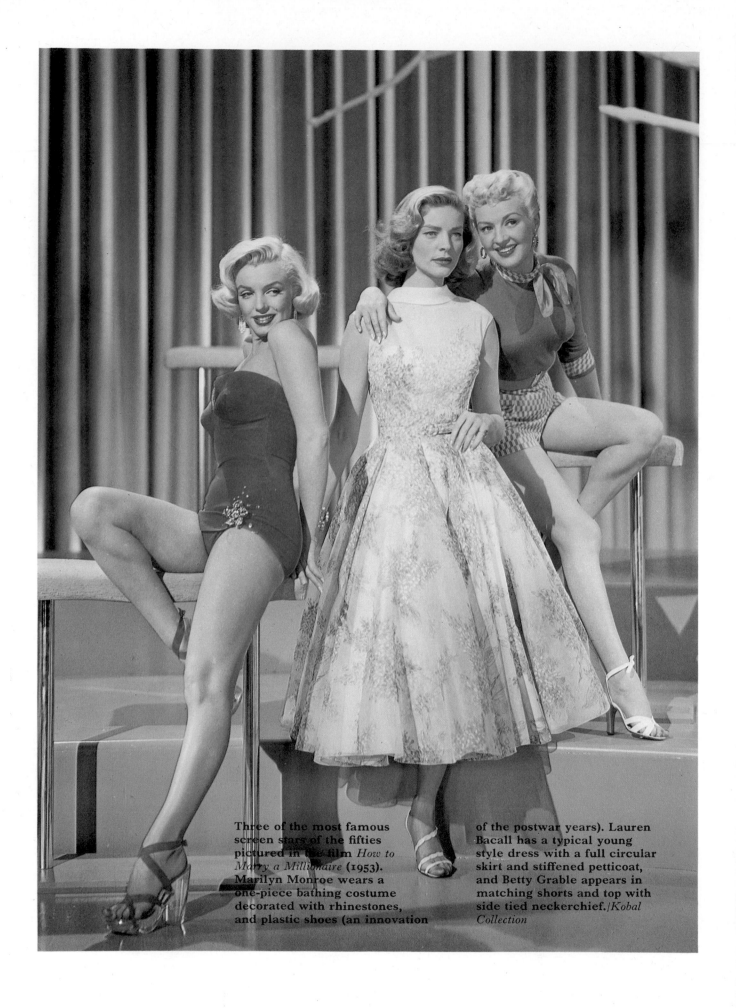

Three of the most famous screen stars of the fifties pictured in the film *How to Marry a Millionaire* (1953). Marilyn Monroe wears a one-piece bathing costume decorated with rhinestones, and plastic shoes (an innovation of the postwar years). Lauren Bacall has a typical young style dress with a full circular skirt and stiffened petticoat, and Betty Grable appears in matching shorts and top with side tied neckerchief./*Kobal Collection*

Sybil Connolly put Irish folk tradition on to the map of *haute couture*. This long flowing felt skirt and velvet bodice is typical of her style (1954)./ *Harper's Bazaar*

A portrait of Elvis Presley in 1957 showing the American tough-guy image./*Kobal Collection*

sometimes engaged for only one performance at a time. The first singer to be mobbed and fêted on a filmstar scale in the early forties had been Frank Sinatra, whose good looks and soulful eyes appealed to women. According to legend, Sinatra's manager paid the bobby soxers $1 (about 25p) each to scream at his first performance, thus initiating the vogue for mass audience hysteria. Other idols were Danny Kaye and Bing Crosby, who were past-masters at the song and dance routine.

In the fifties a slow change was taking place; the romantic crooning of the white singers was beginning to absorb influences from the aggressive beat of Negro rhythm and blues songs. Caution was the keynote of the early stages, for promoters were not sure that the overt sexuality of rhythm and blues would be acceptable to white audiences. The lyrics were severely toned down and the beat was simplified, but the rock rhythm was there and it was just what the teenagers wanted. When Bill Haley and the Comets cut *Rock Around the Clock* in 1954 it became an immediate hit in the United States, spreading rapidly to the rest of the world. It stayed in the pop charts for over a year and sold fifteen million copies. The success of this disc marked the beginning of teenage music, which became known as rock and roll.

The hero who crystallized the new movement was Elvis Presley, who rocked and rolled on stage in a manner calculated to excite his audience. He soon earned himself a nickname he hated, "Elvis the Pelvis", and his hip gyrations were the subject of much scandalized comment. Never before had a white singer brought out the sexuality of his songs in such a blatant manner. Previously sex appeal had been cloaked under the trappings of romanticism and the very word "rock" was a *double entendre*, meaning both dancing and lovemaking which lyricists were careful to use in as seemingly innocent a manner as possible. When Elvis sang the girls in his audience screamed, swooned and fainted, working themselves into an uninhibited frenzy. In the dance halls they jived and rocked, their layered petticoats twirling and swirling in time to the beat. This mass hysteria had an extraordinary effect on clothes: formality was swept away overnight and individual flair became the key to fashion. Elvis himself was a flamboyant dresser, seeing clothes as a part of his sex appeal. Sometimes he appeared in a sweater with tight, hip-hugging jeans; sometimes he drove on stage in a golden Cadillac, stepping out of it to perform in a gold lamé suit, his wrists and shoes glittering with jewelry. His sideburns reached to his earlobes and his hair, heavy with grease, came up in a great ducktail plume off his forehead. Quick to realize his appeal, the Elvis Presley Company brought out a series of accessories for his fans: Elvis perfume, scarves printed with his portrait, belts, jeans,

hats and charm bracelets. Lipsticks in shades named after favourite discs were popular: "Hound-dog Orange", "Heartbreak Hotel Pink" and "Tuttie-fruttie Red". It was the beginning of the vogue for star-inspired accessories on which teenagers dissipated their incomes.

Fancy dressing was a feature of the pop culture and few aspiring singers felt they could do without a fashion gimmick. Wee Willie Harris dyed his hair flaming pink and wore a polka-dot bow tie and baggy candy-striped "Big Bopper" suits with fluorescent shoes. Jerry Lee Lewis sported a pillar-box red suit and marched on stage with a golden comb, which he applied to his hair at intervals. Little Richard wore a baggy suit with elephant trousers with twenty-six inch flares at the bottoms and his hair was backcombed in a monstrous plume like a fountain. His lyrics, like many others bordered on gibberish for it was the energy of his singing and his vital personality that led to his success not the inherent quality of his songs. The fact that a message such as this: "Tuttie fruttie all rootie, tuttie fruttie all rootie, tuttie fruttie all rootie, awopbopaloobop alopbambboom," could achieve hysterical applause shows how far the pop movement was carrying young people from the soupy "I kiss your little hand, madam" of their parents' youth. Their clothing reflected this change.

Like many of the best rocksters, Little Richard came from the southern United States, which throbbed with the sound of black music. Elvis was from Mississipi, Buddy Holly from Texas, Jerry Lee Lewis from Louisiana, Gene Vincent from Virginia, Fats Domino from Lousiana, the Everly Brothers from Kentucky, Charlie Rich from Georgia, Eddie Cochran from Georgia, Chuck Berry grew up in St Louis – the list of heroes was endless. By contrast, the British stars – Cliff Richard, Tommy Steele, Billy Fury, Marty Wilde, Terry Dene, Adam Faith – seemed subdued. Most of them adopted a "youth club" appearance, with sweaters, jeans, striped socks and black leather, though Cliff Richard did start a phase for black shirts and white ties. It was not until the Beatles came on the scene in about 1962-3 that Britain had any significant influence on the pop movement. Their popularity completely changed the look of teenagers, encouraging longer hair and more stylish clothes and adding Parisian touches such as the Cardin lapel-less jacket. The Carnaby Street ethos, which flowered in the sixties, was putting down its root towards the end of the fifties. Bill Green was producing colourful and cheap clothing – velvet suits, trousers made of ticking, prefaded jeans and hipster corduroys. It was the start of fashionable fancy dress, which was taken up more successfully by John Stephen, the man who initiated the vogue for kaleidoscope lighting and blaring pop records, in an attempt to make shopping an amusement rather than a chore. Customers included pop stars such as Cliff Richard and Billy Fury and by 1961 he had four shops – and no less than eighteen two years later.

Following the first wave of rock came a craze for skiffle – a kind of do-it-yourself band requiring no skill except a sense of rhythm, and few proper musical instruments. Thousands of "groups" began to strum on cheap guitars, thump on washboard, dustbin lids and tin pans and blow on paper and combs. In London alone three thousand skiffle groups were active, all singing American-style folk songs (in American accents). Male skifflers affected fringe beards, bold open-necked shirts and corduroy trousers, while the girls cultivated a look of folksy simplicity with loose sweaters, black stockings and long disordered hair.

Black stockinged women and their bearded boy-friends, both clad in polo-neck pullovers, duffel coats and sandals formed the nucleus of the beatnik or Bohemian group, who were recruited mainly from the "progressive" intelligentsia and art-school students. Their heroes were the American writers Jack Kerouac and Allen Ginsberg, who in their own countries had very large followings. They wore anti-dress and their appearance was dictated by the belief, possibly subconscious, that there were more important issues on which to expend one's energies than dress. They tended to hide their figures beneath layers of bulky clothing for all occasions from parties to Nuclear Disarmament marches. Colours were predominantly black or brown, relieved only by pendant jewelry or badges.

The dress of adolescents in the fifties, from the well-dressed teddy boy to the poorly dressed beatnik, reflected the change in young people's attitude to their environment. They were no longer dependent on the tastes and outlook of their elders and had no urge to dress in imitation of them. They had shaken off the yoke and the result was sometimes a shocking flam-boyance and sometimes a less dramatic disregard for the conventions of neatness. Anything that staked out the freedom of the young generation was popular, a generation growing up in an affluent society, inspired and reassured by its own music, the beat of rock and roll.

Far left:
A Neo-Edwardian dressed for Ascot in 1954. The suit shows a narrowing of the line and attention to elegant detail. The pearl pin in the cravat, the wing collar and neatly furled umbrella were standard accessories./*Radio Times Hulton Picture Library*

Fourteen year old teddy boys in 1954 wearing their hair in American crew-cut style. This offended their headmaster, who issued the order; "Get your hair cut English style and don't wear flashy clothes"./*Radio Times Hulton Picture Library*

Teddy boys dressed for a dance
at the Tottenham Royal, North
London, in 1954. Some teds,
like the lad on the left, were
very particular about the care
of their dress, while others,
such as the group on the Far left,
had a more casual approach.
This picture shows the long
drape jacket and the 'slim-jim'
tie./*Radio Times Hulton Picture
Library*

Liberace believed (and still believes) that fancy dressing was part of the performing image and chose colourful jackets, frilled shirts, bow ties and plenty of jewelry./*Metro Goldwyn-Mayer*

Left:
Bing Crosby and Danny Kaye in a song and dance routine from the film *White Christmas* (1951). They are wearing lounge suits with exaggerated detail, large shining lapels to the jackets, studded shirts and cutaway waistcoats./*Paramount Pictures*

Full skirted rock and roll dress by Linzi, 1958./*Sport and General Agency*

Right:
Compared with the previous illustrations, this scene from *Mister Rock and Roll* (1957) exhibits the exuberance of the rock-and-roll movement. The nylon petticoats layered with stiff frills that were then in fashion made this kind of dancing popular probably thanks to the age-old male desire to peep beneath the skirts of his partner./*Paramount Pictures*

Left:
Elvis Presley wearing the jeans and sweater that he popularized. The band wear the Hawaiian flowered shirts that were first worn by performers but later became accepted for office workers in hot climates./ *National Film Archive*

The sportswear designer Ted Tinling created several of Tommy Steele's outfits for his first stage appearance in 1957, among them this rock-and-roll shirt. Listeners wear play clothes embroidered with musical themes, including small figures rocking around a clock and little creatures representing the "See you later, alligator" jingle./*Ted Tinling and Radio Times Hulton Picture Library*

Left:
The same phrase appears on one of these teenage dance dresses made for 1957 jive sessions./*Fox Photos*

Two outfits typical of the student's wardrobe in the late fifties. Black sweater and slim skirt worn with a simple ornament and a candy striped sack dress worn over black stockings and blouse./*Fox Photos*

A scene from *The Subterraneans*,
the film of Kerouac's book and
forerunner of the beatnik style.
The costumes illustrate
symptoms of anti-dress (1956)./
Metro Goldwyn-Mayer

Ban-the-bomb marchers in 1956 wearing duffel coats, baggy anoraks, crumpled jerseys, socks and plimsolls – all features of the beatnik style of careless dress./Camera Press

Sports separates for 1954.
Typical of the period were the
off-the-shoulder tops, with
three-quarter length slacks
worn here by the well-known
Marla Landi. The dress on the
right is a shirtwaister with
wide cynched-in belt./*The John
French Photo Library*

Sports Clothes

Two adjectives were promoted by manufacturers in the fifties to describe clothing with a sportive slant, "casual" and "relaxed", the former being advanced to the status of a noun when applied to footwear. Together the two words signalled the end of the Victorian cult of work, and the beginning of the "new Elizabethan" enthusiasm for sport and leisure.

The traditional sports of the well-to-do were subject to the democratization that was influencing all activities. New materials and techniques, as well as build-it-yourself kits, had created a whole navy of small boatery on all available water stretches, two million people went fishing, three times as many people as before the war were learning to ride horses and skiing was no longer confined to a small body of *cognoscenti*. In addition a multitude of spectator sports required informal clothing for the onlooker. Open-necked shirts, checked trousers and contrasting sports jackets became standard wear for men outside the office and women followed mainline fashion trends, preferring blouses and skirts, trouser suits or pinafore frocks to the more formal dress.

Separates were born as we have seen, in the United States, but it was in Italy, via Italian America, that casual wear achieved its reputation for elegance. Knitwear, which had consisted mainly of shapeless sweaters, was given a new lease of life and was enthusiastically applauded at Brioni's San Remo shows. He experimented with different shapes and fabrics for knitwear – crew-necks and V-necks, shaggy mohair jerseys and cashmere cardigans, reviving traditional designs in his patterned pullovers. A favourite American ensemble, though one that was slow to attract European buyers, was a dress and matching cardigan, the knitted garment lined or trimmed with the dress fabric.

Italy also specialized in attractive ski-clothes and holiday separates – candy-striped shirts and skirts, towelling ponchos and the hand-painted beach clothes and "palazzo pyjamas" in which the designer Pucci delighted. Men at summer resorts wore a "cabana set", which originated in the beach cabanas (holiday clubs).

A jacket was obligatory when they were collecting food and drink from the fashionable clubhouses, so the swimming trunks, which were cut like shorts, acquired a matching jacket. The cabana set was very much in fashion during the fifties. But most beach fashions originated on the French Riviera, particularly at Saint Tropez where the "Union des Créateurs de la Mode Cote d'Azur" staged annual fashion shows that were attended as eagerly as the big collections in Paris. It was there in 1947 that the bikini was launched upon a startled world, though it was too new to alter the appearance of the beaches. Most women still felt safer in the one-piece bloomer bathing suit, which sometimes had a little skirt over the puffed bloomers, while the one-piece swimsuit in all its fanciful versions was the uniform of the beauty queen and filmstar. A collection aimed at millionaires that toured the States attempted to forecast the future in a collection called "Swimsuits for Tomorrow", featuring models such as "Bauble for a Uranium millionaire", a simple suit of classic design paved with thirty pounds of rhinestones; "Diamonds in your Future", covered with pendant crystals and a row of nineteen diamonds across the bosom; "Timed for Tomorrow", a gold aluminium number set with two waterproof watches – though whether even the most voluptuous girl on Long Beach ever saw these confections seems doubtful. The more appealing swimsuits were reserved for 1960, when Rudi Gernreich, America's leading sportswear designer, produced his cutout swimsuits, to be followed in the early sixties by topless beach fashions.

Swimming was a sport that showed off the female shape to alluring advantage; tennis was another. During the forties manly shorts were worn with bulky tops, giving an impression of boxed uniformity. The first major breakthrough came in 1949, when the British designer Ted Tinling dressed "Gorgeous Gussy" Moran for Wimbledon in a fitted frock with matching panties edged with lace. The publicity and discussion that centred round Gussy's clothes on this and subsequent occasions brought the notion of tennis fashions to the fore and once the public outbursts of indignation had receded, the trend initiated by Tinling received worldwide acceptance. He was soon designing outfits for virtually every well-known tennis personality of the fifties, his basic idea being to follow mainline fashion trends. For instance, when the A line crossed the Channel from Paris in 1955 he promptly turned to attractive A line tennis dresses. He was also ahead of the field in exploring the potential of manmade fibres for sports clothes, with the now familiar Terylene pleated tennis skirt originating in his 1953 collection.

Tinling was one of the few couturiers to concentrate on sports clothes. Together with the French designer Pierre Cardin, he influenced standard wear for all branches of sport throughout the world. Interestingly, details they had introduced into sportwear would subsequently be adopted for everyday wear. Tinling was also the first designer to forecast the advent of disposable clothing. He made a sample paper dress for a television programme in 1956 to demonstrate its potential, though it was not until 1961 that he was marketing paper dresses. The idea of expendable clothing was at the bottom of the casual wear movement, since the assumption was that anything could be thrown together with anything else, or could be casually discarded according to the wearer's mood.

The centrepiece of the young wardrobe for both sexes was a pair of blue jeans, which looked as though they were ripe for the old clothes man – a look which was painstakingly cultivated. Teenagers would order their levis direct from the United States, since the real thing could not easily be obtained elsewhere at that date. They would sit in a hot bath wearing their new acquisitions until they fitted like gloves, then hang them out to dry in the sun until they were faded and fray the ends so that they looked worn. The major appeal of levis was that they were one of the very few garments at that time that were inaccessible to the older generation since they were too rough and ready.

Casual clothing was indeed very much the prerogative of the young, for as Hardy Amies recently remarked: "The new is always for the young first. The young will try the untried because they have no fixed ideas." Once their innovations are commonly seen on the backs of the older generation it is time for the picture to change. Thus sportswear and separates are subject to seasonal variations in an attempt to produce new stimuli for the young. The following pictures show only a handful of the many variations that occurred.

The epitome of the casual look was the combination of a skirt with a sweater or blouse, which became the standard daytime uniform in this period. Originally the skirt and blouse idea had been popular as a means of making coupons go further, since a blouse could be run up from an old tablecloth and several garments could be worn in different combinations to ring the changes. The drawings were made in 1947, but the classic line of the skirt hardly changed throughout the period./Harper's Bazaar

Full stiffened skirts worn with shirt blouses in 1957. Big dotted designs were popular with these can-can style skirts. The waist was tightly clasped by a plastic or leather belt. The basket carried by the girl on the left was an innovation that came from Spain, where lunch baskets came to be used as a busy girl's beauty box cum holdall./*The John French Photo Library*

Left:
A cotton skirt and blouse by Ted Tinling, featuring large printed strawberries re-embroidered with sequins. The ensemble was worn by Shauna Trabert, a top model at Chanel, at the Wimbledon finals in 1955./*Ted Tinling*

Dolman sleeves were seen everywhere during the forties and fifties, and were chosen as a reaction to the neatly fitting twinsets popularized by Chanel. The model, with its wide sleeves drawn into a tight waistband, dates from 1948./ *The John French Photo Library*

Far right:
Traditional knitting patterns, such as fairisle, were popular during the war when women had the time to create the complicated patterns. Afterwards the same designs were retained and featured in sporting knitwear. This sweater was made in 1958./ *Handknitting Wool Council*

Right:
A new-style sweater girl wearing the typical "sloppy" jumper of the fifties. This four-foot version made by Dorville in blue Angora and lambs-wool cost £6 ($15)./*The John French Photo Library*

Right:
Fashionable ski clothes were
first seen in the Italian
collections, brightening up the
dull navies and blacks that had
previously been seen on the
slopes. Other countries were
not slow to follow the Italian
lead. This British outfit of 1957
shows a reversible anorak in
glacier blue and citron yellow
with dark navy slimline pants./
The John French Photo Library

Middle:
Another traditional British
pattern (Arran) is used in this
slacks and top outfit of 1958.
During the fifties there was a
popular vogue for sewing
sequins, diamantés and
paillettes on to sweaters to
create a sense of glitter. The
alice band that the model
wears in her hair was very
common, generally being
made of velvet-covered metal
or plastic. The thonged sandals
were inspired by eastern
influences and have remained
popular into the seventies./
Handknitting Wool Council

Far right:
A yachting dress made in
England for the American
market (1956). Typical are the
small boats in the fabric design
which often featured on
clothes for sporting occasions./
Fox Photos

129

The lace-edged panties worn by "Gorgeous Gussie" Moran at Wimbledon in 1949 were caught by photographer Bob Ryder, who was awarded a trophy as Photographer of the Year for this picture. The outfit, designed by Ted Tinling, was the first feminine costume to be seen on court for several years and its hint of eroticism (which to modern eyes seems tame) aroused a furore. A spokesman at Wimbledon announced that the championships would not be permitted to become a ground for fashion parades, but the general public flocked to see what Gussy would wear next and the national press carried the story for days./*Associated Press*

Tennis dresses thereafter followed mainline fashion trends. Here Tinling used a new Terylene mixture to give durable pleats to his A line tennis dresses of 1954. Men's fashions, however, showed no variation from the man pictured here./*Ted Tinling*

Above:
A lady's riding habit (1941). The unusual feature of this pair of jodhpurs is that the side seams make a detour to run down the centre, thus creating a neat tailored appearance. The jacket is made in District checks, its length designed to reach the horse's back./*Tailor and Cutter*

Far left:
Women's golf wear had been dowdy and uninteresting since the First World War. These ensembles were the first brightly coloured and properly fitted outfits to achieve general popularity. They were made in 1953 from a fabric called osmalane a 50/50 cotton and wool mixture produced in the Lancashire mills./*Ted Tinling*

Left:
Men's golf wear varied little from this outfit./*Moss Bros*

Far left:
A cotton beach dress and
skirted playsuit for 1948, printed
in garish multicoloured designs
typical of the time. Central
halter straps were popular./
Camera Press

Left:
A playsuit of 1952 shows how
both the fabric and the cut had
improved. The fabric culls its
inspiration from Japanese
painting, the effect being
reinforced by the paper
parasol./*The John French Photo
Library*

Below:
Although the bikini had made
its appearance on the beaches
in 1947, one-piece bathing suits
were still more popular, many
being strapless. Swimsuits
furnished an excuse for many
exotic or outlandish ideas, such
as this Valentine's Day model
in sequinned towelling worn by
Belinda Lee in 1954./*Ted Tinling*

The leading American designer
of the sixties was Rudi
Gernreich, who produced this
cutaway swimsuit for the
summer of 1960. It is made of
knitted wool, which gives it a
snug fit./*The Wool Bureau Inc*

Above:
Beach clothes included shorts
and shirts, the top generally
hanging over the shorts, as in
this 1949 ensemble by
Horrockses./*Cotton Board*

Right:
Casual wear in 1952. American
girls would wear the spotted
handkerchief tied in a double
knot at the neck. The rolled up
turnups of the denim jeans
were in keeping with the
popularity of the three-quarter
length garments./*The John
French Photo Library*

Two outfits popular with the
huntin, shootin', fishin
country gentleman. Both are
timeless./*Moss Bros*

Two men's sporting outfits, a flowered shirt in Japanese-style fabric and shirt and slacks in the Italian style. The horizontal weave of this emphasizes the squatness of the Italian look./ *Ted Tinling*

Far right:
Knitted cotton was new in 1958, when this bulky blazer-style jacket was made. It is worn with a white tennis shirt and cotton trousers. Slip-on shoes like these were commonly worn with sports clothes./*Ted Tinling and Cotton Board*

Right:
A cabana set (1959) created for the fashionable pools and beaches of the United States, where men were not allowed into the clubhouse in swimwear. The shirt is printed with traveller's cheques in tans, pale yellow and white on a dark grey ground, one of the graphic themes that was popularly used for menswear./ *Ted Tinling*

Hats with veiling like this 1949 version, were sought out by women who wanted to cultivate the soft veiled appearance of the screen heroine./*Mr Z. Ascher*

From Top to Toe

Historically speaking, accessories came first and clothing developed from ornament rather than the other way round, for early man was far more interested in decorating his body so as to assert his superiority over the animal world than in sheltering it from the elements. Decoration in primitive societies consisted – and indeed this still obtains – of body painting, disguising the hair or face, wearing elaborate bead and shell jewelry and painting skins and leathers. All these form the basis of modern accessories: they are essentially superflous, shoes apart, and their main function is to impress. The instinct is so basic that no amount of economic depression could withdraw woman's ability to surround her person with little bags and purses, pretty hats, scarves, jewelry and knick-knacks of all kinds. During the war the British Board of Trade recognized this by making comparatively few restrictions on the supply of accessories; in any case it was impractical to enforce rationing in this field, since most accessories could be made out of almost anything – *papier mâché* would do for a hat-frame, an old tablecloth could become a scarf, a cushion could be converted into an embroidered bag and magazines were full of ideas for making jewelry out of odds and ends, including old film spools. Women had to learn to be good with their hands, as it was most unlikely that they would find any suitable accessories in the shops. Anything that was available tended to be crudely functional and unadorned: bucket bags big enough to hold gas masks and woollen berets to keep the ears warm.

But the accessory industry as a whole soon recovered lost ground; boutiques sprang up in Paris, Florence and Rome to tempt customers with feathers, flowers, kid gloves, parasols, velvet masks, coronets, hair buckles, scatter pins, perfumery and even crystal raindrops glistening on the rose decorating a lady's corsage. In language that waxed lyrical after the last accessory had gone off rationing in 1948, *Vogue* described the kind of attention a woman was expected to give her choice of small items to wear. At lunchtime "you are essentially unfussed, pin-neat and organized.

This is the time of a muff or stole, a single touch of luxury to your city suit . . . immaculate small gloves . . . an exquisite tiny handkerchief, unforgettably, fastidiously white." *Vogue* saw tea as an elegant repast with fragile china and gleaming silver presiding over the hour of feminine gossip. A lady would put a "pretty formality into her dress . . . a delicate shoe . . . perhaps a velvet opera pump . . . a slim small bag avoiding all tendency to bulge, holding your nearest essentials . . . a cardigan sweater, casually soft . . . quiet tones in jewelry, cool pink or coral". Then moving on to the cocktail hour, the time when she could shine, she was advised to "foil it in contrived simplicity . . . choose from a whole drift of dark colours . . . the beautiful off-blacks, plums, raisins, great greens and browns; a subdued background for the elegance of diamonds", offset by the longest glove she could buy. At dinner "a long romantic dress would be worn with period jewelry (perhaps an Edwardian choker or a *Directoire* pendant), the flutter of a fan, rich colour of stoles and shawls and a tiny velvet carry-all holding more than ever in even less space!"

At the top of the accessory list for the fashionable lady was her hat, which was very much a part of the year's silhouette. Hats put the finishing touch to a dress, giving it the look of the season. So last year's suit could be made to look like this year's with a cleverly chosen head covering. The revival of the hat proper was due to Dior, who in 1947 rescued millinery from the state of disarray it had reached during and after the war, when the only law governing design seemed to be to make hats as outrageous as possible. Dior hats crowned the head, echoing the wide sweep of the skirt and giving their wearer confidence, while for Balenciaga's more classical lines the pillbox hat seemed more appropriate. The pillbox indeed became the hat of the fifties and Dior later included it in his repertoire. It was often worn with alluringly feminine veils, with British women going to great lengths to make their own, as veiling proper was unobtainable. Less adventurous women wore felt hats, to which the manufacturers gave homely names such as the Companion, the Roamer and the Polo. These hats have persisted into the seventies as part of the schoolgirl's uniform, though the modern miss is naturally constantly seeking new angles at which to set it to achieve individuality.

As for men, it was generally thought in the forties and fifties that if a young man wanted to get ahead he had to get a hat, in Britain at any rate, the bowler and the umbrella being the traditional symbols of the City gentleman. Men's hats were confined to sober colours – brown and greys and quiet greens – with woodland shades for the town and checked tweed caps for the country.

Women's hats in the fifties repeated traditional outlines, shifting forwards on the head and breaking into cascades of feathery trimmings. Surveying the scene in May 1956, *Punch* noted that there was "less plumage but more blumage", especially roses and lilies of the valley. Then "after flowered hats came the deliciously edible hats: soufflés of whipped up tulle, charlottes of folded organza, *crèmes brûlées* of lacey crinoline-straw. And then the inedible hats, toadstools of black net or swirled georgette, fringed parasol mushrooms and purple-spotted puff balls – instantly fatal." These frothy concoctions were followed by hats shaped like hairdryers or large white drums. But the hat was losing its following, partly because milliners paid little attention to the latest developments in hairdressing and made head-hugging bonnets that spoiled the hairstyle, and partly because the hat gave a note of formality to any occasion and the free-and-easy influence from across the Atlantic disparaged solemnity. In the United States girls insisted that long flowing hair need not be the prerogative of children and that grown women could appear at any social function with glistening hair brushed loose or caught up in a pony-tail (a style that Picasso's painting of Sylvette helped to popularize).

The hair-styling of the fifties marked the first time since the twelfth century that fashionable women had been allowed to reveal a mass of wavy hair without being accused of wantonness, for it was the exotic appeal of hair that had led to the Church's insistence on head covering. Very short hair styled in the "bubble cut" inspired by Ingrid Bergman in *For Whom the Bell Tolls*, a film made at the end of the war, was very popular and short hair remained fashionable throughout the fifties. New soapless shampoos, developed while soap was rationed, encouraged women to grow their hair, as did the range of dyes, tints, lacquers, setting lotions and hair sprays that were flooding the market. Mothers now let their hair hang loose in an effort to recapture their youth, while their contrary daughters would pin it up in what was known as a French pleat to show that they had reached maturity. So a compromise situation was reached in the mid-

fifties, with half up and half down styles consisting of a beehive chignon plus shoulder-length locks.

By 1955 hairdressing had become a boom industry, with 29,827 "salons" in Great Britain alone. New processes were evolved to give apparent bulk and height to the head and this did much to make the wearing of hats both undesirable and unnecessary. The wet hair would be wound round large plastic or horsehair rollers and backcombed when thoroughly dry; the top would then be brushed smooth and the whole edifice sprayed with lacquer. The style achieved Marie Antoinette-type proportions. Techniques of permanent waving had also improved and British women no longer had to suffer the hard-to-arrange coils and pleats of hair that the Board of Trade had tried to popularize during the war.

Hair frames the face and the face has always been the gauge of changing ideas of beauty over the centuries. As *Punch* noted in February 1957, "Of all the accessories to fashion taken chic by chic, it is the face which most truly bestows the contemporary look. A cast of countenance cannot change with the mutations of the mode but there is overlaid on it a fashionable appearance." The fashionable head fell into definite categories – blonde, brunette and redhead, the sexy and the gamine look. Pictures of some of the fashionable beauties of the age have already appeared in this book (pages 95-99 and 158-159). Most famous were Hollywood stars such as Betty Grable, Greer Garson, Lana Turner, Jane Russell and Lauren Bacall in the forties and Marilyn Monroe, Jayne Mansfield, Doris Day, Brigitte Bardot, Sophia Loren, Audrey Hepburn and Leslie Caron in the fifties.

The advent of colour films made an enormous impact on cosmetics, for while previously only the outline had been seen, women soon appreciated the effects that could be created with colour. Their desire to achieve the unblemished appearance of screen stars caused Hollywood cosmetician, Max Factor, to create an everyday version of "pan-cake" make-up to gloss over imperfections. He also brought out a range of eye-shadows and lipsticks. Glossy, filmstar lips could now be imitated with "satinized" lip salve, manufactured by Lancôme in Paris to give an eager "just licked" appearance. (Combined with the garish colours of the forties, this tended to create a distinctly vulgar look.) Later on, in the fifties, innovations in Italy toned down the brightness with titanium, resulting in lips with a pale gleam. The idea was subsequently extended to frosted nail varnishes in pink, silver and evergreen. By the end of the fifties *Vogue* had managed to co-ordinate cosmetic colours with the colours of the season's clothes and publicized shades to match whole outfits. Most magazines were continually publishing advice on make-up, their ideas ranging from one minute thirty-five seconds for the shortest possible *toilette* for the busy mother with a child and other interests to look after, to nineteen minutes twenty seconds for a speedy answer to evening allure.

Scents were popular in France and the United States but were bought less in Britain than in any other fashion-conscious country. This was partly because they had been either rationed or unobtainable for a decade, but also because a puritanical streak in the British character seemed to frown on the idea of luxury items for oneself. The average British woman has never understood what French women learn at a very early age – that the only way to be economical with scent is to be extravagant! Most perfumes in the postwar period were either outrageously expensive or vulgarly cheap; Goya were therefore immediately successful in the fifties, with their medium-priced fragrances such as "Black Rose" and "Passport" for women and "Cedar Wood" for men. As we have seen, the French couture houses were soon gaining much of their revenue from the sale of perfume. It was this alone that kept Chanel going all through the war years and indeed the fall in sales of scent in the United States was the main factor that persuaded her to reopen her fashion house in 1954. The rate of growth of sales of Dior perfumes illustrates the industry's importance, for he launched a separate perfume company in 1947. His first fragrance, Miss Dior, was marketed in Baccarat crystal bottles designed by himself. In the first year a small factory of six hands produced 283 bottles (twenty-five years later eleven million bottles were being turned out by the 700 employees of Dior Perfumes Ltd). Miss Dior, Diorama, Diorissimo and Diorling and the toilet waters Eau Fraîche and Eau Savage were selling all over the world except for China and Albania (but including Siberia).

A facial accessory that achieved unexpected popularity in the fifties was the wearing of spectacles for decorative purposes, though this was not in fact a new idea, since recent discoveries had unearthed Chinese examples that were simply circles of plain glass, presumably intended for ornamental purposes. The spectacles popular in the fifties were made of coloured plastics, sometimes sprayed with glitter dust and inlaid with rhinestones or diamantés, with exaggerated wings at the outer corners. Men could wear heavy horn-rimmed spectacles which conveyed an earnest "family doctor" look, while children had to suffer National Health glasses – and suffer they did, for at that early stage in its career the Health Service did not encourage imaginative designs.

The most expensive accessory was, and is, jewelry, traditionally the most glamorous vehicle of display. During and after the war, little new jewelry was made, so those with money to spare bought Victorian gems, which were unrationed and plentiful. The left lapel of the utility suit was almost always adorned with a Victorian or Edwardian brooch. Then in the late forties the art of jewelry making was revived. The traditional designs of the previous generation were resuscitated, the favourite being diamonds in semi-baroque gold settings, or the new precious metal (for jewelry) of platinum. Asprey and Cartier in London and Paris produced the finest jewelry in this style. Then came a new trend which involved producing jewels that were akin to sculpture, aided by the perfection of wax-casting techniques. Artists such as Picasso, Derain, Cocteau, Braque and Salvador Dali all produced jewels in their own individual styles. The beauty of uncut stones carefully selected and mounted to display their crystal structure was more widely appreciated in the fifties, and large rings began to be fashionable.

Costume jewelry was also popular and manufacturers in Czechoslovakia and East Germany turned out tens of thousands of the same necklace made from brass wires and cut glass stones. During the fifties a craze sprang up for cheap plastic jewelry, particularly for the poppet beads that were in every teenager's jewel box.

This chapter has so far dwelt on the head and shoulders, not surprisingly as the face is the focus of attention and its decoration absorbs most of women's artistic interest. But the figure too was important, for in spite of the popularity of organizations such as the Linda Leigh Large Girls Club (in Britain), the ideal was to be trim and slim. During the war aids to this end were unobtainable and for a long time the ordinary woman lost the habit of controlling unwanted bulges. It was not until the appearance of the A line that it really became necessary to have corsets that fitted the line of the dress and the underwear manufacturers of Britain launched an annual National Corset Week to make women more conscious of their foundations. A new elastic yarn called Laton revolutionized the underwear industry in the fifties, making it possible for the figure to be controlled without the discomfort of the stiff whaleboning of Victorian undergarments. Teenagers wore elastic pantie girdles when pencil-slim skirts were in fashion, the more fanciful being decorated with coloured rhinestones and diamanté stars.

"Lingerie" was a word that came into use during this period and was used to describe all underwear and night garments, which tended to be in plain or frilled nylon for summer and Clydella for winter. French nightwear, as might be expected, showed a greater interest in frills and *frou-frou*, while in Germany the concept of sex appeal in undergarments hardly existed. A fashion from the United States hit teenage bedrooms in about 1957, when knee-length or shorter "baby doll" nightdresses with scooped necklines trimmed with angel lace and baby ribbon appeared in the shops. The pyjamas consisted of gossamer-thin jackets just covering – but no more – brief puffed panties. Baby doll nightwear achieved success even in the cold climates of Oregon or the North of Scotland, which seems to suggest that the desire to attract is stronger than the call of comfort. The older generation, of course, disapproved, since such skimpy garments were suggestive of sexual freedom. The attitude of their authoritarian generation was summarized by the President of the British Board of Film Censors in the late fifties, Herbert Morrison, who said of an X-certificate bedroom scene: "I suppose we shall have to pass it, but men and women don't go to bed together with no clothes on!"

The most sought-after undergarments of erotic appeal were, as has already been noted, nylon stockings, which were being manufactured in bulk in the United States by 1939. Apart from the difficulty in obtaining them they were extremely susceptible to laddering, and although invisible menders did a brisk trade, expenditure on nylons took a large bite out of a career girl's wage packet. Seamless stockings, which appeared on the mass market in 1952, were not popular, largely because they were poorly shaped and so tended to snag more easily. Tinted nylons appeared towards the end of the fifties and were very popular with the young, though it was not until the next decade that coloured and patterned stockings and tights brought legs into the forefront of figure interest.

Leather rationing during the war produced a grave shortage of footwear (requiring in Britain seven coupons out of the precious allowance) and in France the most fashionable shoe shop came out with a line of gaily coloured wooden sabots or clogs. The United States, however, had a fair supply of both raw materials and labour and proved to be creative in the shoe sphere, promoting the use of unfamiliar materials (such as cork and plastics for footwear). Open-toed and open-heeled shoes began their popularity in the United States in the late forties.

The trademark of the fifties' look was a high-heeled shoe, which, as in previous centuries, was connected with sex appeal. The sharply pointed stiletto heels that became the rage in Hollywood and in all fashionable circles all over the world were first seen – as so many new fashions were – in Dior's collection in 1952. A new discovery in the field of metallurgy had made this new development possible, though its destructive potential may not have been foreseen at the time. Had Dior known that airlines would be forced to organize special meeting to discuss ways of making floors resistant to the attack of pin-points of steel hammered into the ground by the weight of thousands of lady travellers, he and his shoe designer Roger Vivier might not have been so anxious to introduce a shoe into the Dior wardrobe. Roger Vivier specialized in producing exquisitely bead-embroidered, lace-covered slipper shoes, which could cost £50 ($280) per pair.

Italy was responsible for the best leather footwear, Ferragamo and Perugia being the best-known names. Italian designers also produced a full range of bags, belts and other leather accessories, which were always a feature of the fashion parades at the Pitti Palace in Florence and were greatly sought after in Europe. Italy showed her leadership in all branches of the accessory trade specializing in the tone of aristocratic chic. The head of the House of Fabiani once summed up the Italian attitude towards clothing: "Each season clothes renew women and therefore the world and each season we earnestly believe that women have never been quite so beautiful nor the world quite so interesting". It is left to the modern woman to decide, on looking through the pictures in this book, how far the fashions of the forties and fifties match up to her idea of the beautiful. The chances are that the gap of appreciation is too close and that the girl of the seventies sees these fashions as ugly, interesting or quaint but rarely beautiful. Even so a nostalgia for the clothing of previous decades is, in the seventies, showing its effect on fashion design and many of the styles shown in this book could be worn at the time of writing without seeming dated.

The British Ministry of Labour issued this poster during the war to ensure that factory workers, especially those working on munitions, would take precautions to keep their hair out of the machinery. The turban at the top of the picture was worn everywhere. Basically it was a scarf folded in a triangle and tied on top of the head, the ends being tucked under. After the war the headscarf, now tied under the chin became fashionable wear for all classes of society./ *Imperial War Museum*

146

be in the fashion - cover your hair

Above:
An evening hat by Dior (1954) with a wide wing span, dipping brim and draped crown. Dior took great pains with his hats, discussing the details with expert milliners and ensuring that the ones he chose complemented the lines of the dress./*Harper's Bazaar*

Far right:
An American Easter bonnet for 1951 enhances the *ingénue* look for which American girls were famed./*Keystone Press Agency*

Right:
French hats after the war were outrageous and many unusual ways of celebrating the end of

the war were thought up./
Keystone Press Agency

Above right:
A small crown hat conforming to the fashion in 1951, using net veiling to give a peacock's tail effect./*Keystone Press Agency*

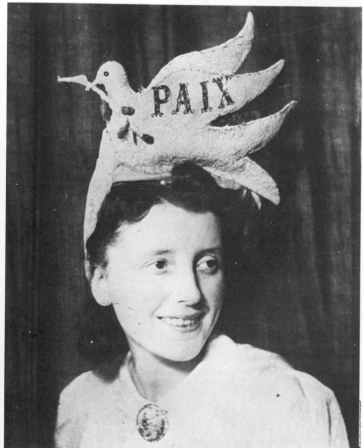

Above left:
A hat by Schiaparelli in printed silk with violet roses and green leaves on a white ground (1955). The Norwegian blue fox stole is by Fath./*Mr Z. Ascher*

Below left:
The late fifties saw the revival of the cloche hat of the twenties. This hat is dated 1957 and has a wide band buckled in front. The large clip earrings, also seen in the picture on this page, were popular with this type of hat./*Camera Press*

Above right:
This photograph was released in 1941 by the British Board of Trade to show girls in the armed services how to style their hair. The neat rows of sausage curls were supposed to be easy to keep in place. Other popular styles were page boy bobs and rolls of hair pinned up on the forehead./*Keystone Press Agency*

Below right:
Part of the army education scheme designed to re-equip girls for civilian life was a course in beauty culture. Here ATS girls are learning how to tint their hair./*Keystone Press Agency*

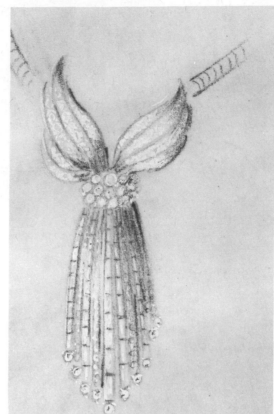

Above:
Three designs by Andrew Grima for brooches in the 1950s. Grima was one of the first designers to use rock formations as the starting-point of his creations, breaking away from the traditional symmetry favoured by the old style court jeweller./*Andrew Grima*

Below:
A style created for Bettina by a leading British hairstylist of the fifties, Steiner, and photographed in Paris in 1956. Steiner had recently introduced a new product called Starmist, which was sprayed onto the hair to lighten it./*Steiner*

152

Above left:
Wingshaped spectacles with
sides decorated with
rhinestones and diamantés.
Fancy glasses had many
different forms at this period.
This pair was designed jointly
by John Cavanagh and Michael
in collaboration with the optical
industry./*Fox Photos*

Below:
Picasso's portrait of Sylvette,
painted in 1954, helped to
popularize the pony tail
hairstyle./*Giraudon*/*SPADEM*

Above right:
A diamond necklace by Cartier
(circa 1950) in traditional style.
The three centre motifs of the
necklace were detachable and
could be worn as clip brooches,
while the outside pair doubled
as earclips. The whole necklace
could also be worn as a head
ornament for gala occasions./
Cartier Ltd

The fashionable face changes through the centuries and famous beauties have always set the fashion for looks. Here are four screen stars of the fifties who, along with the American beauties on page oo, were the pin-ups of the age. Brigitte Bardot, whose charm lay in her smouldering seductiveness, Sophia Loren, subject of more cover photographs than anyone else, Audrey Hepburn, whose gamine looks were the ideal of the younger generation, and Sabrina, the "dumb blonde" who was in the forefront of the cult of vital statistics./*National Film Archive, Paramount Pictures and Unifrance.*

Above left:
A romanticized picture showing a cotton poplin petticoat (1954). The skirt is smooth over the hips and has a full flare from the hipline, creating the body shape required for A line and Y line dresses./*Cotton Board*

Below left:
Model girl Barbara Goalen wears a silk negligée in 1949, the year before she hit the magazine headlines. Well illustrated in this picture are the perfectly manicured hands of the model, lacquered with bright red nail polish./*The John French Photo Library*

Above right:
Nightwear for 1943 still favoured long nightdresses, in spite of rationing. These two crêpe nightdresses were in pastel shades and required six coupons. The multi-striped pyjamas needed eight./*Marshall and Snelgrove*

Below right:
An artificial silk nightdress (1949)./*The John French Photo Library*

Magic

Presto—beautiful lingerie garments like these are magic in these difficult days. Every one is a tonic for your wardrobe . . .

"Claudia." Dainty spotted crêpe Nightdress, cut on the cross, with full Empire bodice held with cords. Peach spot white, sky spot white. **66/5**
(6 coupons)

"Sweet Dreams." Floral crêpe Nightdress, cut on the cross, ideal for washing, as the straps . from shoulder untie which keeps the gown quite flat. It is finished with two small pockets. Coloured grounds of white, sky, pink and peach. **79/9**
(6 coupons)

"The Lisbon Story." Gay tailored multi-striped Pyjamas. The top can be worn as a tunic (as sketch), or tucked in as a blouse, with well fitting trousers. The colours are all bright and animated. **68/-**
(8 coupons)

Lingerie—First Floor

Page Eighteen

157

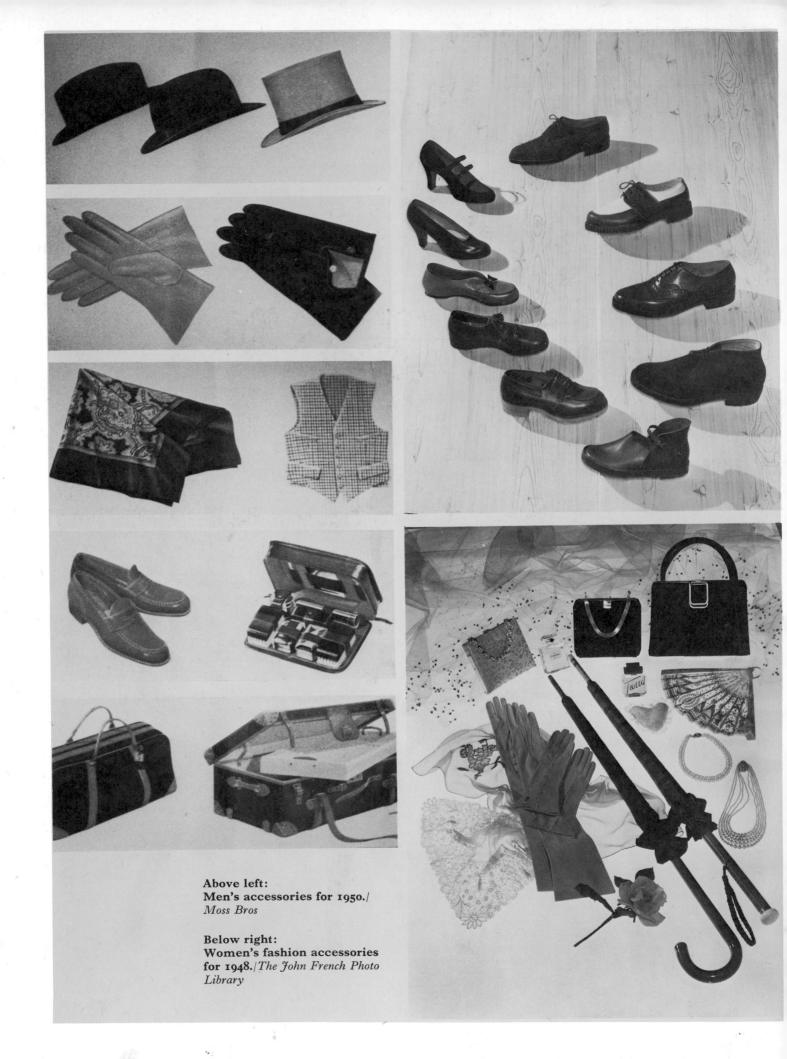

Above left:
Men's accessories for 1950./
Moss Bros

Below right:
Women's fashion accessories
for 1948./*The John French Photo*
Library

Above far left:
Men's and women's utility shoes, designed for comfort and durability since leather was still rationed in 1949. They required as many coupons as a skirt or a pair of trousers in the previous year./*The John French Photo Library*

Below:
A black and white silk evening bag embroidered in red, made in 1954 for Balmain. It conforms to the envelope shape that was popular at this time./*Camera Press*

Above left: \
Shoes for 1954./*The John French Photo Library*

Bottom:
High heels and pointed toes were the mark of the shoes of the fifties and are recorded here in an early Pop Art painting by Allen Jones, *T-riffic.*/*Arthur Tooth and Sons Ltd*

Below middle:
A page of shoes for 1951 made in Italy and London. Descriptions and prices have been left in the picture./ *Marshall and Snelgrove*

it's all in the line . . . of Paris, Italy and London

Here's silhouette. Here's a new scintillating talent. Here's the cream. New designs by the foremost shoemakers in Europe.

Creating models specially for Marshall & Snelgrove. A new group of beautiful shoes for the discriminating. A whole series, elegant without exaggeration, advance fashion for immediate day and evening wear

Fashion Shoe Salon, Ground Floor

**Marshall & Snelgrove
the first name in
Fashion Shoes**

Acknowledgements

Many people have helped me with their memories of fashions in the forties and fifties. I am grateful in particular to James Laver, who kindly read the text for me; Francesca Wolf, who helped me with the picture research; Mrs Vere French and Mr Zika Ascher, who helped me to sort through their archives; Miss Madge Garland, who gave me her memories and ideas for pictures; Vivienne Menkes, who suggested changes to the text, and all my friends who gave me odd pieces of information. My thanks also to Julia Singleton, who typed the manuscript for me.

Select Bibliography

Alburgham, Alison: *View of Fashion* (Allen & Unwin, 1966)
Angeloglou, Maggie: *A History of Make-Up* (Studio Vista, 1965)
Bertin, Celia: *Paris à la Mode* (Gollancz, 1956)
Binder, Pearl: *The Peacock's Tail* (Harrap, 1958)
Cohn, Nik: *Pop from the Beginning* (Weidenfield & Nicolson, 1969)
Cohn, Nik: *Today There Are No Gentlemen* (Weidenfeld & Nicolson, 1971)
Dior, Christian: *Dior by Dior* (Weidenfeld & Nicolson, 1957)
Garland, Madge: *Fashion* (Penguin, 1962)
Garland, Madge: *The Changing Face of Fashion* (Dent, 1972)
Greer, Howard: *Designing Male* (Robert Hale, 1953)
Gregory, James: *The Elvis Presley Story* (Hillman, 1957)
Harper's Bazaar
Hartnell, Norman: *Silver and Gold* (Evans, 1958)
Hopkins, Harry: *The New Look. A Social History of the Forties and Fifties in Great Britain* (Secker & Warburg, 1963)
Lynam, Ruth: *Paris Fashion* (Michael Joseph, 1972)
Picture Post
Punch
Queen
Rees, Norman: *St Michael, A History of Marks & Spencer* (Weidenfeld & Nicolson, 1969)
Sunday Times
Turner Wilcox, R.: *Five Centuries of American Costume* (A. & C. Black, 1963)
Vogue
Woolman, E. and Chase, I.: *Always in Vogue* (Doubleday, Gollancz, 1954)

The publishers are grateful to the following magazines, firms and individuals for releasing copyright material:

Ascher Textiles
Associated Press
Bradleys
Camera Press
Cartier
William and Norma Copley Foundation
Cotton Board
Debenham & Freebody
Dereta
Dior
Disney Productions Ltd
D. H. Evans
Fox Photos
The John French Photo Library
Giraudon and Spadem
Andrew Grima
Goya Perfumes Ltd
Handknitting Wool Council
Harper's Bazaar
Hartnell
Imperial War Museum
International Wool Secretariat
Jacqmar Ltd
Keystone Press Agency
Kobal Collection
Levi Strauss Ltd
London College of Fashion
Metro Goldwyn Mayer
Moss Bros
Moygashel and Springbak
National Film Archive
National Periodical Publications Inc
Paramount Pictures
Mary Quant Ltd
Radio Times Hulton Picture Library
Silk and Rayon Users Association
Sport and General Press Agency
Steiner
Tailor and Cutter
Ted Tinling
Catriona Tomalin
Arthur Tooth & Sons Ltd
Twentieth-Century Fox
Unifrance
United Artists Inc
Wool Bureau Inc
Warner Brothers